National Theatre

Guide

by Sarah Hemming

PUBLISHED BY NATIONAL THEATRE PUBLISHING
The Royal National Theatre, Upper Ground, South Bank, London
SE1 9PX

First edition published 2019.

A catalogue record for this book is available from the British Library.

Printed and bound in the UK by Cantate Communications.

Typeset by Alan Craig, Kerrypress Ltd, St Albans, Herts.

Designed by Bastian Mueller, National Theatre Graphic Design Studio.

ISBN 978-0-9572259-3-0 paperback

Contents

Act One – Making a Theatre

Act Two – Making a Show

Foreword

In *The National Theatre Guide*, Sarah Hemming offers a privileged backstage tour of the National Theatre, from the actors' dressing rooms to the scenic assembly workshops. Along the way, she demonstrates the huge variety of different jobs that go in to creating our productions. Every show involves a tremendous number of people all working together in order to tell a story on stage because, ultimately, that's what the National Theatre exists to do: tell stories.

This is a place where stories are conceived, nurtured and shared, and – as you're about to find out – everybody on a production feeds in to that process in a different way. Playwrights create the script, giving us settings, characters, plot. Directors, designers and actors take that script off the page and realise it as a living thing. Costume-makers, make-up artists, scenic artists and prop-makers realise the world in which the play takes place. Lighting and sound teams deepen both story and setting, creating atmosphere and effects. A host of other different roles – too many to name here – support and feed in to the work in myriad ways, using a mixture of tried and tested traditional skills and innovative new techniques. You will find out about many of those in this book, too.

We believe storytelling is an important and powerful force, especially when it happens in the live, communal setting of theatre. It allows and encourages us to consider other perspectives; to approach issues and ideas in new ways; to walk in other people's shoes. We believe that as well as being exciting and entertaining, that exercise in empathy is essential for a healthy society.

We want as many people as possible to have that experience, and while this book focuses on what goes on in the theatres, rehearsal spaces and workshops of our South Bank home, we try to live up to the 'national' in our name is by ensuring that people outside of London get to see our work as well – through tours and transfers all over Britain and the world; through National Theatre Live, which beams productions live to cinemas all over the globe; and through Learning initiatives like Connections and Public Acts which invite both young people and adults to become theatre-makers themselves.

So, whether you know the National Theatre and our work well, or whether you are visiting for the first time, we hope you'll enjoy discovering how we bring our stories alive. We hope you'll have the chance to experience some of them, too – both now and in the future.

Rufus Norris and Lisa Burger
Director and Executive Director of the National Theatre

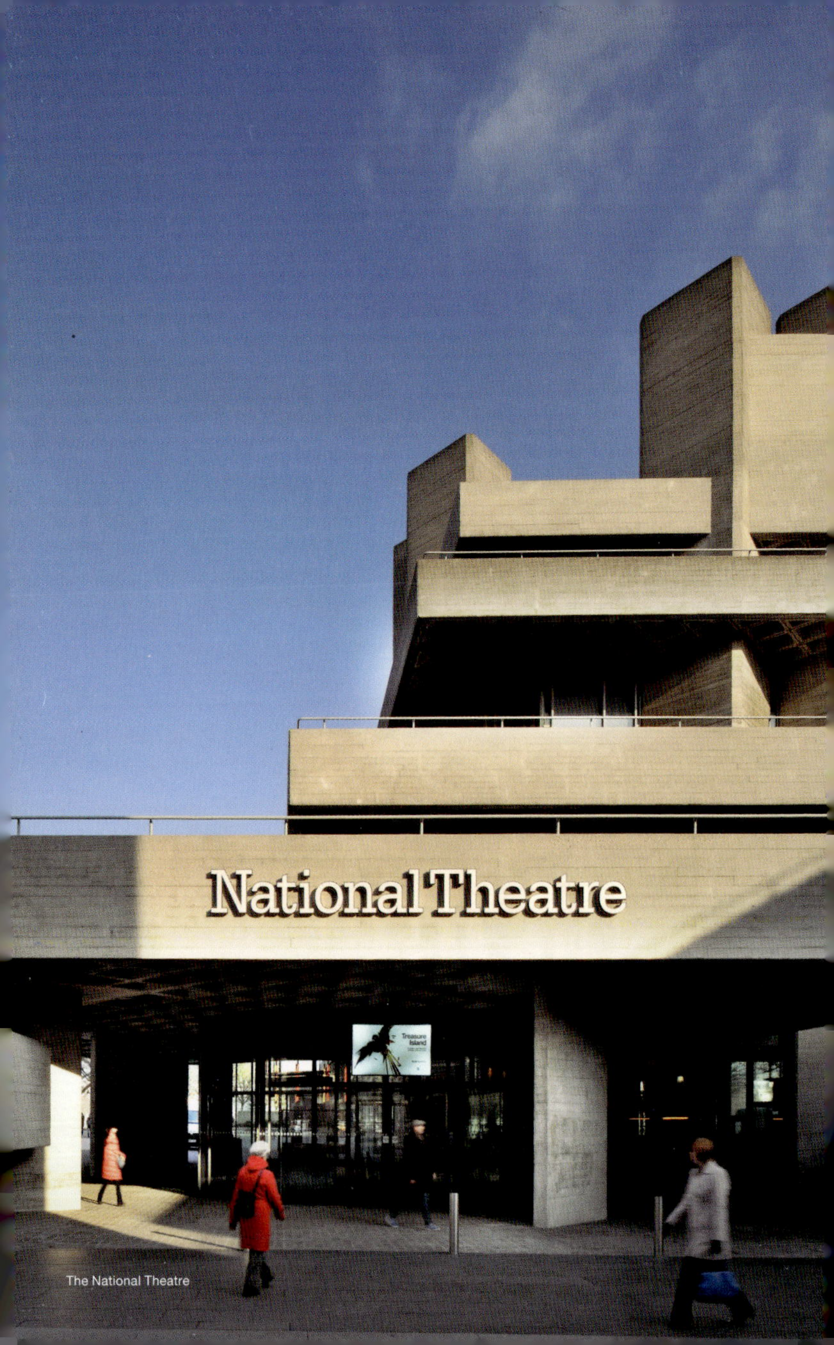

The National Theatre

1.

The Property of the Nation

The beginnings

The National Theatre was an idea long before it was a building. The theatre is now one of the United Kingdom's flagship venues. An impressive concrete edifice on the bank of the River Thames, it is home to three auditoriums, employs over 1,000 staff and stages dozens of plays every year. From here the NT sends touring shows out around the UK and internationally, runs nationwide programmes for children and young people, broadcasts live theatre to thousands of cinemas across the world and coordinates a whole host of other activity. It's impossible to imagine either the physical landscape of London or the theatrical landscape of Britain without it. But for decades – centuries even – it was a distant dream, cherished by those who found it inconceivable that the land that had produced Shakespeare had no national playhouse dedicated to his craft.

In 1848, London publisher Effingham Wilson was the first to call for a national theatre, in a pamphlet entitled 'A House for Shakespeare'. But it would be another century before a law would be passed releasing funds for the building of a national theatre (1949), 115 years before the National Theatre company would launch (1963) and a further 13 years (1976) before the dedicated building – now so synonymous with the institution – would be opened to the public. The NT's passage into full, concrete existence is a rollercoaster story of ups and downs, deals and delays, and the sheer passion of obstinate, optimistic, remarkable individuals.

An impressive list of early advocates for a national theatre includes the novelist Charles Dickens, the poet and critic Matthew Arnold, the politician Winston Churchill and the playwright George Bernard Shaw, who even wrote a play (*The Dark Lady of the Sonnets*) in which Shakespeare puts the case for a national theatre to Queen Elizabeth I.

One particularly passionate voice was the playwright Harley Granville-Barker. In 1904, together with critic William Archer, he drew up a blueprint called 'Scheme & Estimates for a National Theatre', which was published in 1907. Their remarkably detailed plans included everything from a proposed repertoire to company size, wages, seating capacity and seat prices. They joined forces with a committee planning a memorial to Shakespeare, generated funds and excitement, and found a site behind the British Museum. The outbreak of the First World War, however, brought plans to a halt.

Granville-Barker took up the cause again after the war, with the young publisher Geoffrey Whitworth, founder of the British Drama League, also mounting a vigorous campaign. By 1937 the money had been found for a theatre, this time opposite the Victoria and Albert Museum in Kensington. Sir Edward Lutyens, illustrious architect of dignified war memorials, together with theatre and cinema architect Cecil Masey, drew up designs for a grand, classical palace – but then the Second World War meant the plans had to be shelved again.

Parliament decides

In 1949, parliament finally passed the National Theatre Act, authorising £1 million of public funds for the building of a national theatre on the South Bank. In 1951, the foundation stone was laid by Her Majesty Queen Elizabeth (later the Queen Mother). But as plans changed, so did the site – several times – prompting a joke that the foundation stone should be mounted on castors.

At last, on 9 August 1962, Laurence Olivier was appointed Director of the National Theatre. In Olivier, the infant National had not just a leading actor at the helm, but a celebrity and a consummate man of the theatre. Olivier gathered around him some of the leading actors and directors of his day, as well as that famously trenchant theatre critic Kenneth Tynan, who went on to play a huge role in selecting the theatre's repertoire of plays.

Now the National Theatre had a Director, a company, but as yet no bespoke building. Nonetheless, no-one was in a mood to wait any longer. The fledgling company was offered the use of the Old Vic by the governors of the theatre, and promptly moved in to the theatre beside Waterloo Station. It remained there for the first 13 years of its life. The auditorium itself was an elegant space with a proscenium arch – the traditional 'picture frame' style of stage. The offices, however, were anything but glamorous: a line of Nissan huts in nearby Aquinas Street, with a little canteen serving home-made food and a cigarette machine that, rather fittingly, sold only Benson & Hedges' Olivier Cigarettes.

It was from this heady mix of the sophisticated and the makeshift that the NT created its first productions. On 22 October, 1963, it was finally launched with a production of *Hamlet*, Shakespeare's great tragedy, starring the young Peter O'Toole (who had just triumphed as Lawrence of Arabia in David Lean's epic film).

Many of the actors from those early seasons went on to become household names: Maggie Smith, Derek Jacobi, Ian McKellen, Michael Gambon and Joan Plowright among them. Classic plays rubbed shoulders with incisive new work, responding to a new appetite and ambition for plays that reflected the period as one of social change. For Peter Nichols' *The National Health*, which depicted patients on an NHS ward, the stage was sprayed with antiseptic to give the whole production an authentic hospital smell. There were bold gambles too, including an all-male staging of Shakespeare's *As You Like It* and a playful philosophical *Hamlet* spin-off called *Rosencrantz and Guildenstern Are Dead* from a young writer by the name of Tom Stoppard.

Meanwhile the building was slowly coming into being. At around the same time that O'Toole was playing Hamlet, architect Denys Lasdun also made his entrance. He was the man who would design the now-iconic iteration of the building which would actually be built. In 1967 the building plans were unveiled and in 1969 the ground-breaking ceremony for the building finally took place.

The site, Prince's Meadow, near a 90-degree bend in the River Thames, was not exactly a desirable one. Far from the bustling West End, it had been bombed during the war, was boggy, down-at-heel and full of disused warehouses. It wasn't until the 1990s that the river walkway was extended, allowing the South Bank to become the thriving cultural hub that it is now.

Just as the efforts to settle on a site and endow the project with funds had been beset by obstacles and setbacks, so too was the erection of the building. The optimism of the 1960s gave way to the industrial unrest that would characterise the 1970s. Delays and industrial action dogged the construction. Peter Hall, who took over as Director in 1973, kept writing 'official opening' in his diary, then having to cross it through due to further postponements. Eventually he decided simply to move into the unfinished building as soon as one of the three auditoriums, the Lyttelton, was usable.

The move to the South Bank

In 1975 the company finally shifted from the Old Vic to the incomplete National Theatre on the South Bank and in March 1976, *Hamlet* was back (this time with Albert Finney uttering the immortal lines) to mark the opening of the Lyttelton Theatre. The Olivier Theatre opened in October and, finally, on 25 October 1976, the Queen officially opened the whole National Theatre, bringing into being the long-held dream. Laurence Olivier gave a speech of welcome: the first and last time he would ever set foot on the stage of the theatre named after him.

The problems that accompanied the NT's arrival should not overshadow the enormous achievement it represented. The new theatre was an ambitious, optimistic and unique undertaking – bigger, with its three auditoriums and huge number of staff, than anything in Europe or America. It was inspiring too in its egalitarian determination to create a whole new model of theatre-making, with spacious foyers, multiple bars, cafes and toilets for audiences; workshops, offices, dressing rooms and rehearsal spaces for staff – the idea being that everyone, from artistic director to wig-maker to audience member, would be under one roof.

Over the years, the National Theatre has continued to experience both triumphs and tribulations and it has never stood still. It has staged popular hits, such as *One Man, Two Guvnors*, *The History Boys*, *The Curious Incident of the Dog in the Night-Time*, *This House* and *An Inspector Calls*; terrific musicals, such as *Guys and Dolls* and *Follies*; great classical drama such *Richard III*, *The Oresteia*, *Henry V*, *King Lear* (with Ian Holm), *Antony and Cleopatra* (with Anthony Hopkins and Judi Dench, with Alan Rickman and Helen Mirren, and with Ralph Fiennes and Sophie Okonedo) and *The Tempest* (with John Gielgud). It has premiered daring new work – such as *No Man's Land*, *Equus*, *London Road*, *House and Garden*, *Copenhagen*, *Closer*, *Pravda*, *Arcadia*, *The Madness of George III*, *Here We Go* and *Downstate* – and state-of-the-nation plays, such as the David Hare trilogy (about the church, the law and politics) and later *Stuff Happens*. It has launched hugely successful family shows – from *The Wind in the Willows* to *His Dark Materials* to *War Horse* – and weathered controversies (*Single Spies*, *The Romans in Britain*, *England People Very Nice* and *Jerry Springer: The Opera*).

The National Theatre's history and the drama on its stages have reflected the changing social and political fabric of Britain. It has woven itself into the nation's cultural life, continuing to interrogate both elements of its name: what it means to make 'theatre' and what it means to be 'national'. Successive Directors have worked to increase its reach and its remit, introducing cheap ticket schemes, extending the lives of successful shows by sending them into the West End, increasing touring and co-productions with theatres around the country, and developing National Theatre Live – live broadcasts to cinemas both nation and world-wide – so those unable to travel in person to the building or touring venues can still access the work.

The NT now stages around 25 shows a year: since 1963 it has produced over 900. There are still rows, controversies, unexpected hits and unexpected flops – but that is unsurprising for a theatre whose very existence is a testament to passion, obstinacy, faith and hard work. For all the highs and lows on its journey so far, it does, for the most part, continue to aim towards something like Harley Granville-Barker's inclusive vision for it over a century ago:

'The National Theatre … must bulk large in the social and intellectual life of London… It must not ever have the air of appealing to a specifically literate and cultured class. It must be visibly and unmistakably a popular institution, making a large appeal to the whole community … It will be seen that the Theatre we propose would be a National Theatre in this sense, that it would be from the first conditionally – and, in the event of success, would become absolutely – the property of the nation.'

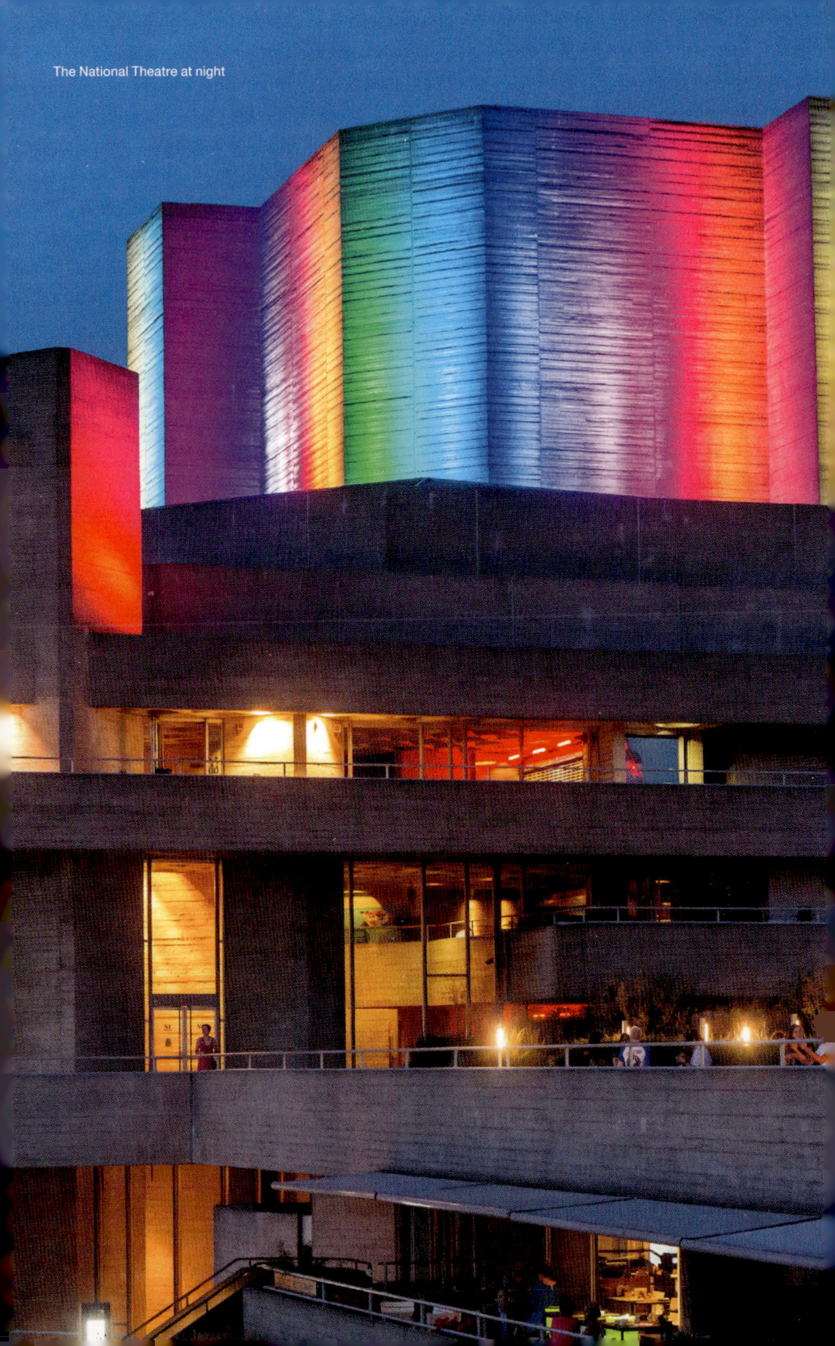

The National Theatre at night

2.

A Creative Hub – The Building

The plan

If you've seen the National Theatre building, you probably have an opinion about it. Everybody does. Rising from the river bank, its bold and stark silhouette is unmistakeable – an extraordinary, vigorous and daring creation. From the moment it was unveiled, it provoked startlingly different reactions. Some people love its striking form and clean simplicity; others find it brooding and austere. On a sunny day it becomes a remarkable and intriguing piece of cubist sculpture, animated by audiences strolling on the terraces between shows; in the rain the damp concrete can look dispiriting.

For the poet John Betjeman, it was a 'lovely work' – even unfinished, the building took his breath away: 'I gasped with delight at the cube of your theatre in the pale blue sky,' he wrote to the architect, Denys Lasdun, having seen the work-in-progress from Waterloo Bridge. Author Simon Jenkins hailed it as 'a masterpiece of British architecture'. For Prince Charles, on the other hand, it was 'a clever way of building a nuclear power station in the middle of London without anyone objecting.' It is unique, a seminal piece of Modernist architecture and, quite literally, the concrete expression of a philosophy about theatre. Denys Lasdun wanted nothing less than a transformation of the theatre-going experience. His plan was to break away from the sort of theatres that defined the West End – the handsome but ornate Edwardian playhouses with their cramped foyers and bars, hierarchical layers of seating, gilded pillars, chandeliers and red plush – and create something more egalitarian and open in keeping with the 1960s spirit of change.

The aim was to build a creative factory where rehearsal rooms, scenic workshops, costume departments, dressing rooms, offices, stages, foyers, cafés, bars and shops would all be under one roof. It needed to be modern and forward-looking, but keep faith with tradition, fuse informality with seriousness of intent and offer a home to both Shakespeare and experimental new work. In the three auditoriums, the focus would be on the drama, rather than on the décor; in the foyers and on the terraces, the emphasis would be on the visiting audiences.

So, the fact that it doesn't look much like a conventional playhouse is deliberate. The National Theatre, Lasdun said, would not be a 'temple with a door', but a building with multiple entrances to encourage people to wander in and take a look. Foyers would be ample and spacious, enabling people to mingle and to avoid the interval-crush. The theatre would be open all day, enabling passers-by to drop in, meet, hang out – even sit on the floor of the foyer. Outside, terraces would cascade down the building, avoiding a monolithic frontage and offering further spaces to gather and even to perform.

For all its scale and size, the theatre would be first and foremost about human interaction. During the design process, Lasdun had a photograph on his wall of a group of spectators gathered to watch an open-air performance in the Piazza San Marco in Venice: it reminded him that people will congregate in any open space to watch theatre. The plainness of the NT design is purposeful. Just as a play is, in a sense, only half-finished when written, and needs actors and audience to bring it to life, so too Lasdun's building is deliberately incomplete without people.

'I don't want anything to come between people experiencing the theatre and your drama,' he would say to the theatre's second Director, Peter Hall. 'It [the building] must just be space, walls, light. And the ornaments of the building are people moving around.'

The man

Even Lasdun's entrance into the National Theatre story was dramatic. While other architects competing for the job arrived at the interviews in October 1963 with a team of assistants and experts, Lasdun walked in alone. It was 'very theatrical' recalled Laurence Olivier: 'Denys Lasdun made an immediate impression by coming in unaccompanied … He seemed to carry with him a quiet conviction.'

Lasdun then announced that he had never previously designed a theatre. He saw this startling admission as a bonus, rather than a problem, and the Building Committee agreed with him. He undertook to start without preconceived notions of what the theatre should look like and argued that the most important aspect of the building was 'spiritual'.

The director Peter Brook, who was on the committee, recalled in a 2013 BBC *Arena* programme Lasdun's 'quiet authority and conviction'. 'We all looked at each other and said, "That's the man",' Brook said. On 22 November 1963, Lasdun was announced as the architect who would design the National Theatre.

Born in September 1914, Lasdun trained at the Architectural Association School of Architecture in London, where he was one of a pioneering and optimistic generation of young architects inspired by the Modernist movement. His work was driven by idealism and the possibilities offered by a new, post-war society: he saw the role of the architect to be the creation of physical environments that would support a decent way of life for people. But he also had considerable respect for classical architects, such as Nicholas Hawksmoor, whose early 18th-churches play such a role in London's landscape. He drew on other traditions, too. The ziggurat form that features in some of his work was seen in ancient Mesopotamia and the student accommodation blocks he designed for the University of East Anglia reflect to some extent the composition of pretty little Italian hill-top towns, which flow down the slopes in terraces. He conceived of modern buildings in their settings as 'urban landscape'.

In the National Theatre, Lasdun was able to bring together the principles of the architectural developments of which he was a part and the innovations sweeping through the arts as a whole. This was the era of hippies, Woodstock, rock music and revolution. Theatre in the 1960s had already seen the impact of 'angry young men', such as playwright John Osborne, ushering in plays about social issues, and it had embraced experimentation such as theatrical 'happenings', (innovative, boundary-blurring performance art pieces that sought to open up new forms of artistic practice). The decade would end with the abolition in Britain of official theatre censorship and examples of counterculture such as the musical *Hair*, with its famous nudity scene. The NT would need to reflect its times, while simultaneously drawing on the great theatrical tradition it inherited.

Lasdun determined to start with the basic facts. 'I told the committee we were going to work from the centre outwards,' he recalled later. 'That meant asking – and trying to answer "What is the relationship between actor and audience, between actor and actor, and between audience and audience?" We looked back [to antiquity] ... and forward to a contemporary view of society, in which all could have a fair chance to see, hear and share in the collective experience of exploring human truths.'

That sense of tradition revisited, of simultaneously looking both backwards and forwards, runs through the building – perhaps nowhere more so than in the Olivier Theatre. Lasdun intended the NT to be a place that took art seriously, but that was also open to all.

The location

Historically the south bank of the Thames was always the scruffy side – the maverick, colourful, bustling, disreputable side, where, in

Shakespeare's day, you could find theatres, taverns, gambling dens, bear-baiting, prisons and brothels. The area, then known as the 'Liberty of the Clink', was beyond the jurisdiction of the City of London, so activities forbidden elsewhere flourished here (hence the playhouses, gambling and brothels). By the 1960s, it had become a far less vivid place, home to a rundown conglomeration of warehouses, disused industries and bombsites, though The Festival of Britain in 1951 had begun a fightback and left a legacy in the shape of the contemporary Royal Festival Hall.

Even so, the area finally designated for the new National Theatre was unprepossessing: a disused bombsite sandwiched between a newspaper depot and Waterloo Bridge. The river walkway that now extends from the building to the East, past Tate Modern and Shakespeare's Globe, had yet to be built: no such festive space existed when the National was erected and the edge of the river-bank was closer to the building (it was extended out to house the walkway). The river too, in the 1960s, was a much less attractive sight, with none of the pleasure-craft or cruise boats you see now. All in all the South Bank certainly wasn't a playful place that families and tourists would head to on a sunny Sunday afternoon, for a stroll past landmark buildings, street performers, ice-cream vendors and food outlets, as they do today.

But Lasdun was undaunted – quite the reverse, in fact. He had initially been commissioned to build a joint theatre and opera house a little further west along the river-bank (in the area now occupied by Jubilee Gardens). When, after much prevarication, funding for the opera house was withdrawn by government in 1966, the location of the project was moved downstream to the current location. Lasdun described the new spot as 'a magical position'. His theatre would be pitched next to Waterloo Bridge with the Houses of Parliament across the river upstream, St Paul's Cathedral downstream and Somerset House directly opposite.

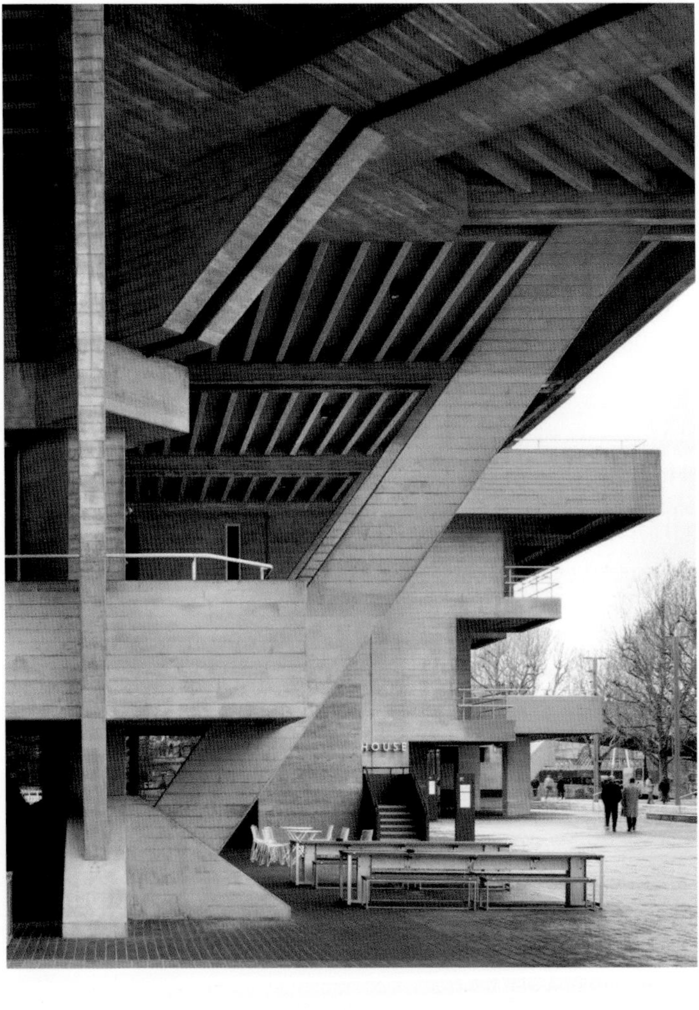

Detail of the north-east corner of the building

The Exterior

Lasdun's final design for the building took account of the presence of Waterloo Bridge; rather than do the perhaps obvious thing, and face the river square on, the National is set on an axis that runs South-East to North-West, with a line running from the sweet spot on the theatre's biggest stage, the Olivier, through the building towards the bridge and across the river towards the church spire of St Martin in the Fields. Stand on the corner of one of the outside terraces, facing towards the bridge, and you feel almost as if you are on the prow of an ocean-going liner, with its layered decks behind you. The multiple terraces and the entrances to them, at several levels, deliberately blur the edges between the building and the surrounding city, and the handrails on the terraces even echo those on Waterloo Bridge, delivering on Lasdun's belief in 'urban landscape'.

You'll search hard for a curve. The building is composed of right angles and diagonals, of soaring vertical lines and strata of horizontal planes. The two fly towers of the Olivier and Lyttelton theatres dominate the outside of the building, with two smaller sets of towers serving to circulate air and mark the building's entrance. There is something of the castle about the structure, but the tiers of terraces soften the effect, swirling around the building like outspread skirts, descending in waves to the river. Its monumental scale and craggy, gradually broadening shape also brings to mind a mountain, perhaps again in tune with that idea of urban landscape. The recessed fenestration makes for dark spaces between the terraces, emphasising the stratification.

Meanwhile the concrete itself is textured, each plank shaped by wooden boards, clamped close to the concrete in a press as it dried. This exacting and arduous job was done by hand. Carpenters made the wooden presses, poured in liquid concrete – sand, water, gravel, cement – left it to set and then removed the wooden shutters. The wood was carefully selected to make a good impression, and no board of could be used more than twice. Close attention was paid to the way the concrete planks would work together and how they would meet at corners or at intersections with staircases, bricks and columns. This process, as so much else about the design and building of the NT, is brilliantly described in Patrick Dillon's book *Concrete Reality.*

Dillon describes how the same care was taken with the colour. Lasdun and his team took pains over the composition of the concrete, choosing a specific ratio of ordinary cement to white cement and selecting a particular sand. The resulting colour is quite a subtle grey, more muddy than metallic, in harmony, perhaps, with the nearby river.

Like so much else to do with the National, the concrete, so often maligned, is a deliberate mixture of old and new. Early enthusiasts of the material were the ancient Romans – both the Colosseum and Pantheon in Rome were built largely of concrete (the latter still boasts the largest unreinforced concrete dome in the world) – and the exactitude of craft involved in texturing and managing the National's concrete planks stands in stark contrast to factory-produced materials. They retain the imprint of long-gone organic matter – wood – and reflect the human labour and ingenuity involved in making them.

The resulting building is deliberately unfussy – in keeping with Lasdun's ethos of unpretentious accessibility – feels modern and urban, but has a soaring, abstract grandeur.

The interior

After many arguments, artistic ructions and changes of plan, the final building was destined to house three auditoriums: a large space with an open stage, a medium-sized space with a traditional proscenium-arch stage and a smaller studio for more experimental work. Lasdun's solution to accommodating all three was to arrange the structure in tiers, with the whole design cascading out and down from the biggest theatre, the

Olivier, and the foyers of the two main houses staggered, on different floors, to offset congestion.

Throughout the building Lasdun plays with angles. Rather than have the three auditoriums stacked simply on top of one another, ranged side-by-side or at right-angles, he faces the Lyttelton squarely towards the river-front while tilting the Olivier at a 45-degree angle. The architecture of their two foyers then mingles, creating an unexpected dynamic within the building. In the Lyttelton foyer, for instance, the coffered ceiling stretches across the space, its lines pursuing a diagonal to the walls, following the rules of the Olivier above it. The smallest space, the Dorfman, sits behind and beneath the backstage area of the Olivier.

Beneath the whole structure lies the car park, now smaller than it was at construction. At that time, a road encircled the building, so that drivers could drop passengers off under a *porte-cochère* at the entrance and drive on down the ramps to park their vehicle underground for the duration of the show. Today, visitors are more likely to arrive by public transport and the surrounding area has transformed into a pedestrian piazza. The approach to the theatre's main door is now made on foot, rather than by car, while the slightly smaller parking capacity created space, in the theatre's 2015 refurbishment, for engineering workshops, kitchens, store rooms and office space.

And just as the outside terraces deliberately blend with the surrounding walkways, pavements and the bridge, so too the internal and external spaces merge. The lines of the exterior balconies continue inside, with a series of landings, and the layered feel extends both inside and out. It's a structure full of changing views and perspectives, full of intriguing geometric shapes and spaces. Huge floor-to-ceiling stretches of fenestration offer glimpses of London as you move about the building, again emphasising its place in the city. And as theatre-goers and visitors roam around the foyers, up and down the staircases, and peer over the balconies or down through the tiny arrow slits on the stairwells, they are constantly aware of their companions throughout the building – meeting, eating, drinking, browsing, queueing. Audiences for one show can gaze down or up at audiences for another as they come and go.

Pass through in the daytime and you will find a quiet hum of activity: a couple of old friends catching up; a huddle of creative artists poring over their notebooks; individuals nursing a coffee as they polish up their play or presentation on their laptops; students taking advantage of the Wi-Fi; a gaggle of visitors on a guided tour; matinee-goers grabbing a bite to eat pre-show. Arrive early evening and you'll see people getting their programmes and drinks; people eating; people meeting.

Meanwhile the job of looking after the theatre's audiences and visitors falls to the 22 front-of-house staff, who can be assisting up to 2000 people a night. 'We've had people who have wanted to propose at a show and people who have climbed up onto the stage,' explains Front of House manager, Stephen Hayes. 'It's not unusual for people to faint: it's warm, they may be tired or hungry, they perhaps had a glass of wine before the show – they faint. It often looks worse than it is. We have medically trained, serving members of the fire service who are our first line squad in those situations – there is one attached to every performance and an emergency number we can call for a rapid response. At the end of the evening, you really notice the differing moods of the audience based on the content of the play. Sometimes they come out effervescent with joy; sometimes really thoughtful or upset. If it's a really difficult subject matter (*Oedipus*, for example) there are two types of people: one group heads straight for the bar, the other heads straight out of the door!'

An open building

By 1976, the construction of the new National Theatre on the South Bank had become so vexed, late, and over budget that Peter Hall decided to move the company from the Old Vic, regardless of whether the new building was ready or not. The Lyttelton opened first, and I directed the first production to originate there, Howard Brenton's *Weapons of Happiness*. As we staggered through a 96-hour technical rehearsal, with scenery crashing, lights flickering, and fly towers failing, I began to doubt his wisdom. But it was also Peter who resolved that the foyers should be open to all-comers all day. He argued that the whole nation had paid for the building, and they were entitled to see into it and enjoy it without having to buy a ticket for a show. Typical of the man: typical of his openness, typical of his generosity, typical of his vision.

— David Hare, playwright

This space – and the opportunity for people-watching that it creates – was crucial to Lasdun: a deliberate celebration of the shared, live nature of theatre. He would talk about the public spaces in the theatre being the 'fourth auditorium' and he saw the movement of audiences – flowing in at around 7pm and out again at around 10pm – as mirroring the tidal movement of the nearby River Thames.

The textured concrete also continues within the building, once again blurring the distinction between inside and outside. The palette of colours (the original carpet was designed by Lasdun's wife, Susan) hints at a natural landscape. The décor is plain, but the geometric patterns and detailed intersections between walls, ceilings and pillars are striking. Spaces are sculpted and lit dramatically to create pools of light and illuminate groups of visitors, as if they were on stage under the spotlights. And although Lasdun obstinately turned away from anything ornamental and ornate, he did aim for a sense of occasion – the symmetrical double staircases which rise up to the Olivier create the feeling of making an entrance.

So, the importance of the audience in live theatre is a fundamental condition of the building. It is deliberately shaped to make visitors aware of one another, both in the foyers and the auditoriums – above all in the Olivier, where the open stage and semi-circular sweep of the seats celebrates the communality of theatre and the audience's vital role in bringing a play to life.

The factory

Just as theatre needs both audience and actors, it needs a combination of imagination and practicality. Lasdun's challenge in designing the National was not just to accommodate the theatres and the desired foyer space, but to deliver on the idea of a creative factory, housing every element of theatre from offices for administration to rehearsal space and dressing rooms, from scenic and costume workshops to catering facilities. The workshops occupy the rear, or south, of the building connected by an internal road to the three theatres so that sets can be moved straight from the assembly area onto the stages. Meanwhile the offices range along the riverfront of the building at the downstream end, wrapping around the Olivier fly-tower, and the rehearsal rooms and dressing rooms nestle at the centre, away from public gaze, arranged around a central light-well and within easy access of all three stages.

The style of the workshop block is more functional than the public areas – composed of brick and concrete and lit by skylights. Here the sets and props that support dozens of productions every year are constructed.

On the roof, nestling between the skylights, are housed another set of industrious workers: the bees that make honey from the plants in the terrace gardens (you can buy the honey in the NT Bookshop, when it is in stock).

And anyone who finds Lasdun's theatre a little sombre can wander round to the back and seek out a small architectural joke. Throughout the building there are no standard windows at all – the glazing comprises recessed floor-to-ceiling glass walls and doors – except on the back wall, facing the road that cuts between the theatre and Waterloo Station. Here there are indeed four small windows. They are cut into the wall like the numerous arrow-slits you will spot all over the foyer – only these particular arrow-slits deliver light to the armoury.

In a sense, the building has grown into itself. Two refurbishments have developed on Lasdun's original idea. Meanwhile the surrounding area has been regenerated to create the sort of festive space and atmosphere he had hoped for, and Shakespeare's Globe, the Bridge Theatre and Tate Modern have since arrived on the South Bank to add to the sense of cultural activity.

The first renovation to take place was carried out by the architecture practice Stanton Williams and was completed in 1998. Most significantly it removed the road that ran round the building, making space for the theatre square in front of it, and so for the beginnings of the more informal gathering and performance space Lasdun had envisaged. In 2007, the exterior lighting was replaced with colour-changing LEDs, which brighten both the building and the area at night.

NT Future, a more substantive refurbishment by architects Haworth Tompkins was completed in 2015 at a cost of £83 million. This has regenerated the building, making it brighter, expanding on the principles of accessibility and inclusion and increasing both workshop space and food and drink facilities for audiences.

The result gives a far more open feel to the whole building, and improves the link between the riverfront and the Dorfman Theatre entrance. Where previously you would have to stroll past the bins on your way to see a show in that auditorium, now you pass people eating and drinking outside. The Dorfman itself – formerly the Cottesloe – has undergone quite a transformation (see Chapter 5) to expand the capacity, ease up some of the pressure in the bar and foyer, which was previously something of a scrum, and house the Clore Learning Centre.

NT Future also saw the addition of a brand-new building: the Max Rayne Centre, located at the back of the theatre on its south-east corner, next to the Dorfman. This new structure, clad in aluminium and steel, is intended to complement the original building, rather than copy it, and houses a huge new Scenic Studio (where the sets are painted), together with other workshops and departments relocated from elsewhere in the building.

A glazed wall on one side of the building encourages passers-by to peep in at the work going on inside, as does the new Sherling Backstage Walkway, accessible from the Dorfman Theatre foyer, which allows the public to peer down on the activity below in the scenic studio and other scenic workshops. This idea of opening up the work-space to the public expands on Lasdun's instinct for accessibility, acknowledges the craftsmanship involved in creating dozens of complex sets a year and responds to a growing public enthusiasm for seeing how creative projects are put together.

Lasdun was knighted in 1976 and was awarded the Royal Institute of British Architects Gold Medal in 1977. The building itself was given a Grade II* heritage listing in 1994. There are those who still dislike it, find it dour or despise the concrete. But approach it on a sunny day, with audiences milling around it and with visitors strolling by along the river walkway, and you can see how Lasdun's remarkable building has become, as he hoped, a democratic hive of activity and a key player in the redeveloped and re-energised South Bank, now a cultural hub in London.

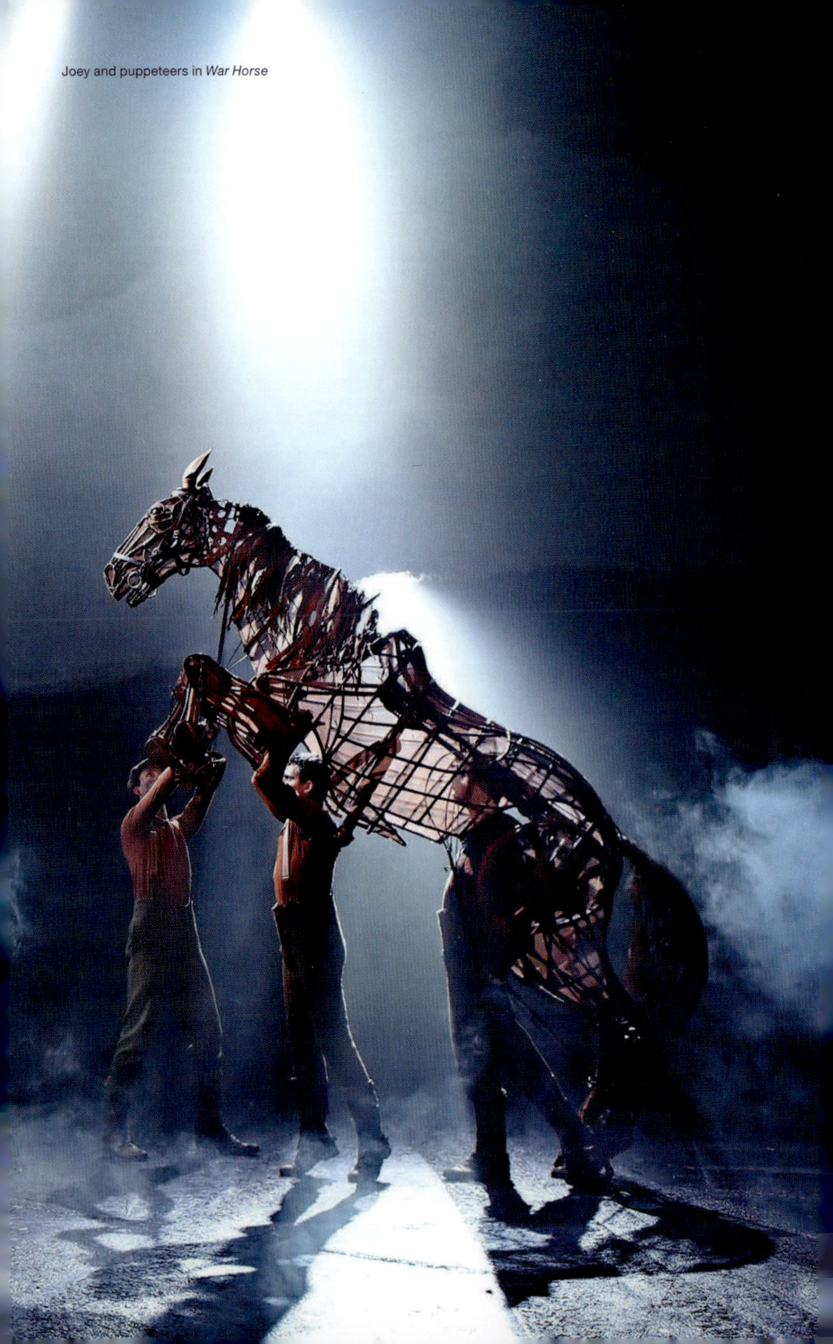

Joey and puppeteers in *War Horse*

3.
The Olivier Theatre

No other theatre like it

The Olivier Theatre is a masterpiece of reconciled contradictions: scale and intimacy; antiquity and modernity; grandeur and simplicity. This auditorium, named after the theatre's first Director, is the largest of the National's three playing spaces and the heart of the building: its fly-tower soars above the theatre, its foyer commands a view of the Thames and its gracious, semi-circular sweep of seats around an open stage is captivating. Step into it, even when it is empty, and you feel a sense of expectancy.

Inspired by the open-air ancient Greek theatre at Epidaurus, the Olivier exemplifies many of Lasdun's driving design principles. It determinedly focuses attention onto the stage rather than the auditorium, combines classical rigour with sleek modernity – no gilded cherubs or fancy chandeliers here – and, above all, it celebrates the audience. It is deliberately non-hierarchical: one of the defining properties of the Olivier is that, no matter where you sit, you can see your fellow audience members.

That mix of scale and communality means that it's the stage best suited to epic work. Here, more than anywhere, you feel the potential for theatre as a public forum and remember that the art-form emerged from the early democracy of ancient Greece. Expansive drama flourishes here, such as Peter Hall's 1981 staging of Aeschylus's *Oresteia*, Nicholas Hytner's pulsating contemporary take on Shakespeare's *Henry V* in 2003, and the 2019 adaptation of Andrea Levy's searing novel *Small Island*.

Its expanse means it can be tricky to play – Albert Finney likened it to performing in the open air. It's an immensely challenging space for a writer, a director or an actor to control. But get it right and you can hold the whole audience in the palm of your hand.

As with so much at the National, however, the Olivier's passage into life was turbulent. From the outset, the NT Building Committee argued passionately about the nature of the theatre's main space, some in favour of an open stage and others preferring a proscenium arch. Lasdun made and discarded dozens of models. 'If you really care about the unity of audience and actor, this means a room,' he said, at one point, arguing for simplicity and against the sort of complex technology that might come between the action and the audience. And, in essence, that is what he designed.

Ancient and modern

The seats in the Olivier rise in a wide, open bowl around the front half of the circular stage, fanning out towards the back wall, which encircles the whole auditorium like a protective arm. The open stage invites direct engagement with the audience. It's far smaller than its vast ancient predecessor at Epidaurus (which holds 14,000 to the Olivier's 1,150) and, while the seats in the Greek theatre wrap around the circular stage for a full 180 degrees, the span of the Olivier auditorium is much narrower – a half-opened fan rather than one at full span.

But the parameters of that fan are precise, fluting out from the centre of the stage in a triangular block to an angle of 118 degrees. This is no accident. 118 degrees is the average range of human peripheral vision. So, from the 'point of command' on stage an actor can face front and address the whole audience without turning their head and the spectators, in return, can all see both of the actor's eyes.

The steep rake of the seating, set into two tiers, also aims to give everyone a clear view and no seat is further than 21 metres from the stage. The design is practical, then, but it also expresses loftier aims. Though he deliberately steered clear of the red plush and stucco that characterises Edwardian West End playhouses, Lasdun wanted the theatre to have a suggestion of ceremony and purpose. The upholstery is purple: the colour favoured by Roman nobility (and, incidentally, Laurence Olivier's favourite shade – he even had a specially commissioned purple London taxi). It's also the colour of the heather that grows around Epidaurus. That natural palette likewise inspires the rest of the décor, with the textured concrete walls echoing the Greek stone and the rich brown carpet representing the earth – the whole intended as a subtle, contemporary response to that ancient Greek hillside.

But, in contrast to the theatre at Epidaurus, this classical simplicity has to function for a contemporary audience with modern expectations. The Olivier needs to deliver sophisticated lighting and subtle scene changes. It must also accommodate a busy repertory programme that demands entire set changes every week or two.

An ingenious mix of backstage systems enables the theatre to store sets for all the shows in the repertoire at the same time. First, and most significant, is the extraordinary 'drum revolve': a unique, purpose-built contraption beneath the stage. A series of shutters separates the stage from the rear stage, where sets on wheels can be kept for quick access. And the huge fly-tower, rising 30 metres above the stage, has enough space to house a London double-decker bus (not that any set designer has taken advantage of that fact – yet) and boasts 180 hoist points to move elements of scenery in and out from above.

The 'flying' machinery in the Olivier is complex and highly automated, using state-of-the-art and custom-made software. Throughout every performance, the automation technician is stationed on a platform half-way up the fly-tower, able to control and coordinate set changes with

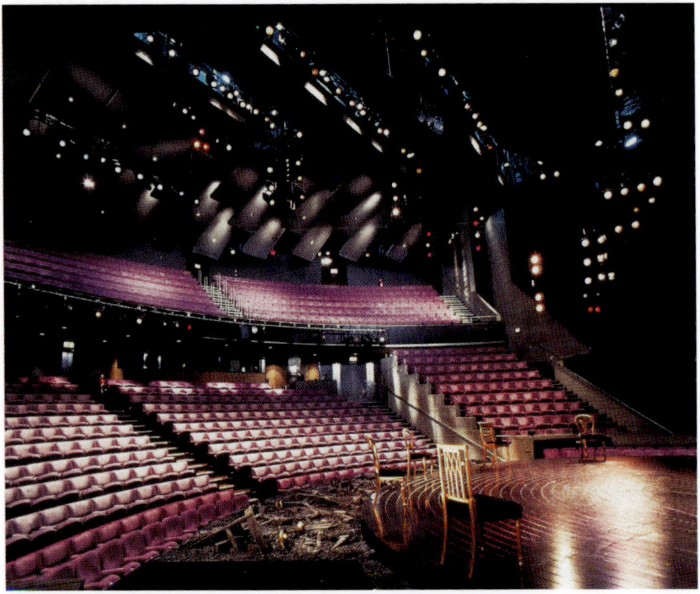

The Olivier auditorium

the touch of a computer screen. A dedicated rigging team look after all the winches, ropes, and 'flown' scenery; they also manufacture, splice and make the rope. There's real pride and care in this rope-work: for the theatre's 2014 staging of *Treasure Island*, the team employed their expertise to ensure that all the on-stage ship's ropes were exactly as they would have been on a real schooner.

Directing in the Olivier

It's a challenging arena because it is not like any other theatre. It's not Greek – it feels it but it doesn't have the same simplicity. And it's peculiar because everybody can see the floor – which sounds like nothing but dictates a relationship between the horizontal and the vertical. There are lots of sound and lighting complications in there. It's a big public arena, so there are some plays that work in there and some that don't. For writers and directors it's a huge jump – there is no other theatre like it. I would say, having done eight or nine shows in there, that whatever you do in the rehearsal room has to be completely remade when you get into the theatre. It catches you out every time – you really have to wrestle with it. But when you get it right the results can be spectacular.

— Rufus Norris, Director of the National Theatre

The opening

The Olivier finally opened to the public on 4 October, 1976, with *Tamburlaine the Great*, starring Albert Finney and directed by Hall. The theatre's birth had been protracted and painful, bound up with the off-stage delays, contractual problems and industrial action that accompanied the whole building's construction. Indeed, the company had been rehearsing Marlowe's classic tragedy since April, 'I was a juvenile lead when I joined this production,' joked Albert Finney, while another actor, Gawn Grainger, wryly pointed out that at the time of the first rehearsal his wife had told him she was pregnant and by the time the production finally saw the light of day, their son had been born.

On 25 October, Her Majesty the Queen officially opened the whole building, attending a production of Goldoni's *Il Campiello* in the Olivier. Since then the Olivier has hosted many of the theatre's most striking shows – as well as several of its more controversial productions. It was here, for instance, that Howard Brenton's *Romans in Britain* played in 1980, including a scene that depicted an attempted homosexual rape which led self-appointed moral guardian Mrs Mary Whitehouse to bring a private prosecution for obscenity against its director Michael Bogdanov (despite the fact that she had not seen the play). At the subsequent trial in 1982, the prosecution was dropped after three days, following a stage-worthy scenario in which the defence had to demonstrate in the Old Bailey that what had in fact been on view had been the actor's thumb, rather than any other part of his anatomy.

The whole affair was farcical in some ways, but it was an exceedingly stressful ordeal for those involved, particularly Bogdanov who faced a potential prison sentence if convicted. It was a significant moment too for theatre history: an attempt to continue the controlling impulse of the censor (a role officially abolished in 1968) had been defeated.

It was in the Olivier too that Richard Eyre's stunning production of *Guys and Dolls* had its premiere in 1982, the first musical the theatre had staged. Its appearance raised eyebrows in some quarters at the time: critical voices suggested that such a populist show was beneath the dignity of the National Theatre. But it was destined to become both a critical and commercial success.

Guys and Dolls lit up that open stage and auditorium – literally, filling the place with pulsing neon lights – and used the communality of the theatre to create an exhilarating evening. Much later, in 2015, Rufus Norris' production of *wonder.land* (which relocated the story of *Alice in Wonderland* to an online game) made equally impressive use of light and sound, taking advantage of the size and scope of the theatre by introducing spectacular, moving video-projections that reproduced the elasticity of cyberspace on a grand scale.

In contrast, *Stuff Happens*, in 2004, exemplified the use of the space as a public forum to discuss matters of great political significance. On a near-empty stage this epic piece by playwright David Hare explored the events that led up to the 2003 Iraq War, mixing fictionalised accounts of private meetings with verbatim extracts from speeches and public meetings and depicting world leaders such as George W Bush and Tony Blair. It emphasised the role the National Theatre, and the Olivier stage in particular, could play in discussing and debating issues of national importance.

It was here in the Olivier that Joey, the equine puppet at the centre of the heart-breaking show *War Horse*, first made his entrance in 2007. That show too was a risk for the theatre: an adaptation of children's novel about the life of a horse during World War One that would rely on a non-speaking creature made of cane and fabric to carry the story and hold the audience. The odds against it succeeding might have deterred even the most reckless of gamblers. But Joey would go on to gallop round the world and become a key player in the theatre's economic fortunes.

And in August 2018, over 200 ordinary members of the public took to the stage to join a small core of professional actors in presenting Shakespeare's *Pericles*: the first production in the National's Public Acts initiative, designed to celebrate and invite participation, and deliberately staged on the theatre's most epic, communal stage.

Stepping up

One of my most thrilling moments was when I directed *The Ramayana* for Birmingham Rep and found out that it was transferring to the Olivier Theatre. It was early in my career and a dream come true. However, I also unwittingly ended up making my stage debut. It was first preview and I was in the audience, when I got ushered out to be told that one of my actors had had an accident and wouldn't be able to continue the performance. We had no understudies. It was me or the show had to stop. There was no time to think and no choice. Throughout rehearsals I had been telling them to be bold and brave, and now it was my comeuppance… I remember stepping out and feeling utterly terrified when I saw the audience, I tried to back off… So not only did I direct in the Olivier, but I performed…

— Indhu Rubasingham, director

A secret weapon

Anyone visiting the Olivier Theatre may be struck by a curious fact – you have to climb several sets of stairs to arrive at stalls level. Why? The answer lies hidden beneath the stage: the drum revolve. It's vast, it's revolutionary – in more ways than one – and it's the theatre's secret weapon.

The drum revolve is an ingenious, five-storey-deep contraption especially created for the Olivier to facilitate swift scene changes without breaking up the integrity of the wide, open stage. Many theatres have revolving stages – flat discs that rotate in the centre of the space – but nowhere else in Europe, except at the Burgtheater in Vienna, will you find a spinning cylinder that allows sets to emerge, as if by magic, from deep below the stage.

The drum works by using two semi-circular elevators, both housed within the cylinder beneath the stage. Called 'Red' and 'Blue', in honour of their colours, they can travel up and down within the well. To change a scene, the crew operating the drum send the set currently on stage on, say, the Red elevator down through floor, leaving a semi-circular aperture on stage. They then spin the whole drum through 180 degrees, so the elevators swap places, and bring the other, Blue elevator with the new set back up through the hole. The top of the elevator can either be level with the stage, so forming a flat surface – like a dinner plate – on which the set sits, or it can rise further up through the aperture to deliver a multi-layered design.

With that set in place, and the play continuing on-stage, the team far below can then install another new set on the submerged Red elevator, ready to repeat the manoeuvre in reverse. The whole operation takes under a minute. And it is not just objects that travel up and down: actors too can sink into the ground or emerge from the depths below – an exhilarating, if slightly nerve-racking experience for the performers.

The effect can be stunning: in the 2014 Christmas show *Treasure Island*, a whole ship in cross-section appeared to rise up onto the stage, with a deck and sails above (on top of the elevator) and a warren of fully-fitted, precisely detailed cabins below (within the body of the elevator). The result was like slicing a 19th-century working ship in half and peering inside. Recent advances in technology have allowed the Olivier's technical team to install new software that enables staff to synchronise the elevators' movement with that of flown equipment. So, as that *Treasure Island* ship rose up through the stage, the telescopic mast, complete with rigging, was simultaneously drawn out to its full height by a winch – rather like a giant ship in a bottle. It was a thrilling sight that vividly expressed the excitement of setting sail on the high seas, and could only have been achieved by having drum revolve and winch working in unison.

So huge is the drum and its attendant machinery that it descends deep below the stage (hence the climb to the stalls). The base of it is the lowest point of the National Theatre – at sub-basement level, beneath even the underground car park. The entire theatre is wrapped around the can-shaped device, which had to be custom built. Peer down into it, and you are confronted with a complex web of ironwork, as robust and elegant as that in a Victorian railway station.

The brain-child of lighting and technical expert Richard Pilbrow and engineer and consultant Richard Brett, the drum revolve was startlingly innovative for its time. That very originality, however, led to problems in getting it to work as planned. It started life in 1978 operating simply as a hoist for scenery between shows and was only used in performance as if it were a more conventional revolve: that is, as a flat rotating platform at stage level.

It wasn't until a whole decade later that it finally came into its own and deployed the elevators as planned. In 1988, designer William Dudley decided, boldly, to use it for his set for Dion Boucicault's *The Shaughran*.

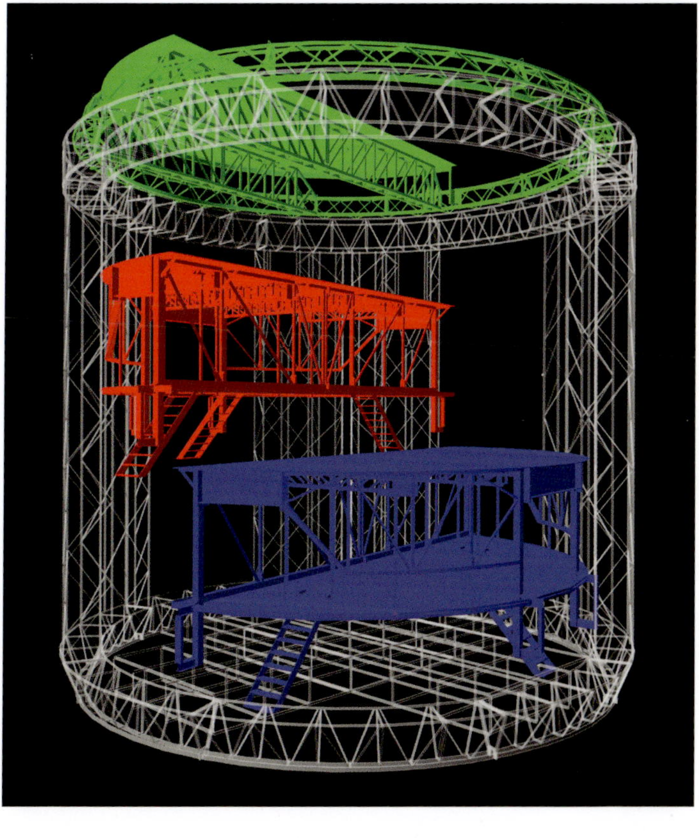

Diagram of the Olivier drum revolve

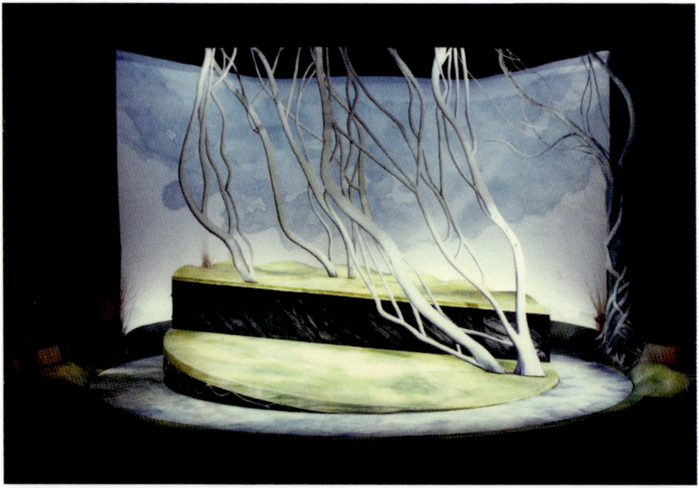

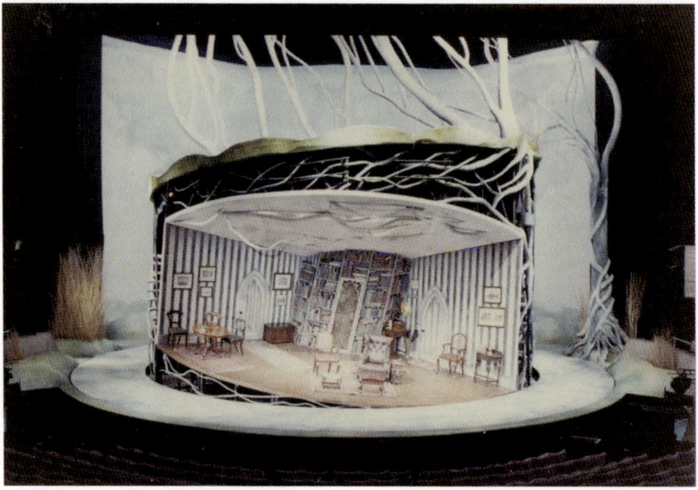

The drum revolve in use in *The Wind in the Willows* (1990)

He designed fabulous settings of extravagant rocky ruins, ivy-clad arches and peasant cottages that would rise from the depths, swathed in swirling mist, as the stage whirled round. The result astounded audiences and critics and set the mood for Boucicault's wild, fantastical period melodrama.

Since then, multiple directors and designers have used the possibilities offered by the drum revolve to solve practical problems of changing sets quickly but above all to enhance the drama. Another hit was *The Wind in the Willows*, Nicholas Hytner's 1990 staging of the popular children's book. In that show, to the audience's delight, Mark Thompson's design excavated the woodland creatures' underground homes – Mole's humble dwelling; Ratty's ship-shape lair – sending each little house up from below. Much less cosily, in 2007 *War Horse* used the structure to create a hellish vision of the trenches on the Western Front during World War One.

The drum revolve can also be used to sculpt the shape of the stage. Drop one of the elevators down and you can create a semi-circular chasm on stage – as used by Paul Brown in *Emperor and Galilean* (2011). Add a further platform and you can raise part of the stage at a pitched angle, as in Rae Smith's design for *Saint Joan* (2007). Use the whole disc as a rotating circle and you can vividly suggest contrasting experiences in one space – as Soutra Gilmour did in *Les Blancs*: a searing staging of Lorraine Hansberry's play about the impact of colonialism in Africa (2016).

It hasn't always run smoothly, but repairs, improvements and the installation of 21st-century operating systems have produced a much more reliable and flexible piece of equipment. Indeed, so innovative and visionary was the drum revolve that ideal support systems have only come into play decades after its initial construction, meaning that it is only now beginning to fulfil its extraordinary potential.

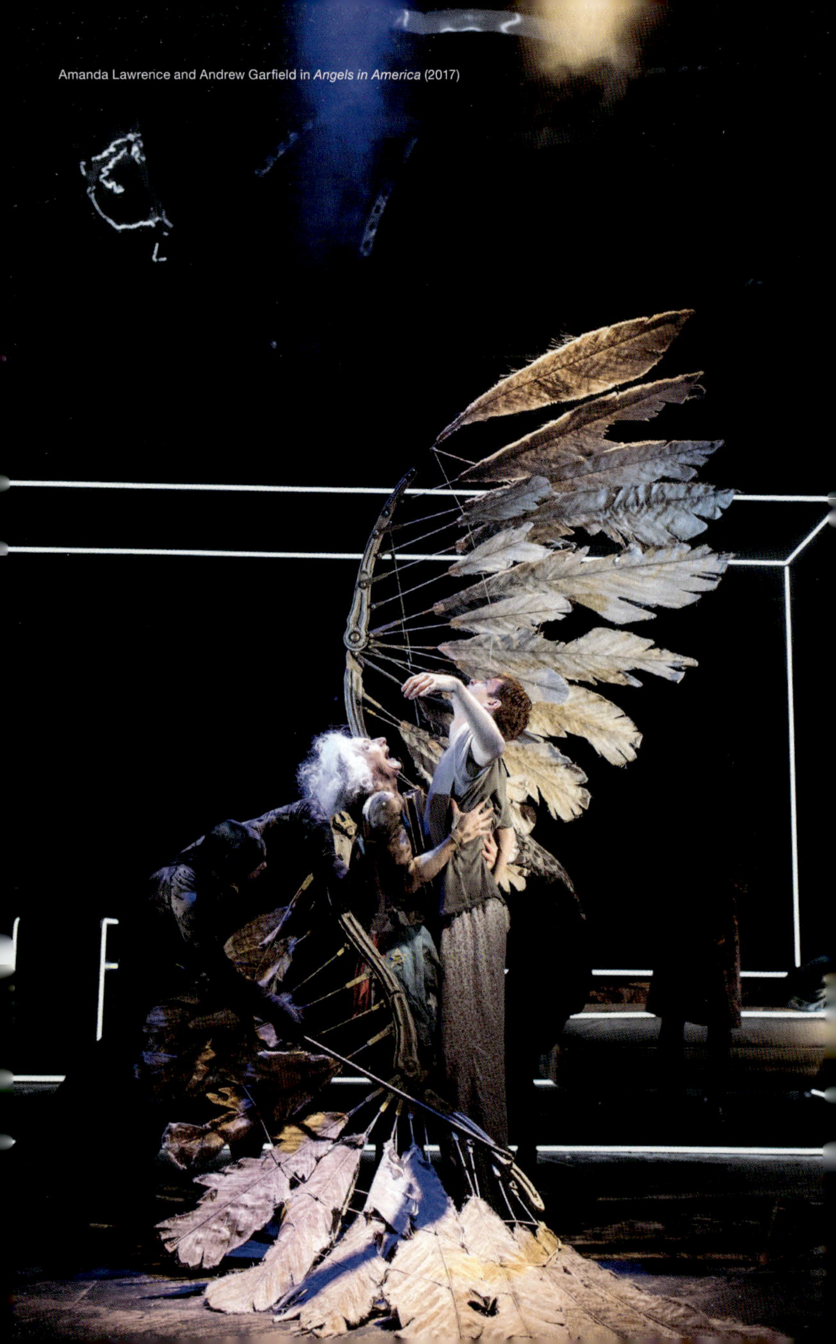

Amanda Lawrence and Andrew Garfield in *Angels in America* (2017)

4.
The Lyttelton Theatre

Framing the art

The Lyttelton is the middle-sized and, in one sense, the most conventional of the National Theatre's three spaces. Named after the Lyttelton family (Oliver Lyttelton, Viscount Chandos was the theatre's first chairman) it has more in common with a traditional West End theatre than either of its neighbours, the Olivier and the Dorfman. It has a proscenium arch framing a rectangular stage and two blocks of seats arranged as stalls (holding 550) and a circle (holding 342).

But there the link with convention ends. As with the Olivier, it is a frill-free zone: you won't find the red velvet, chandeliers and ornate carvings common to many playhouses. With its plain walls and dun-coloured seats, it is deliberately unostentatious, again reflecting Lasdun's desire to focus audience attention on the stage, rather than on the auditorium. There are no pillars to block sightlines and the acoustics are sharp. It feels extraordinarily wide, partly because it is – the stage is unusually expansive (14 metres across), and the seating stretches to match that breadth – and partly because it has no centre aisle. Those wide, continuous rows of seats (up to 36 in a row) are intended to maximise capacity and also to give the best viewing spots in the house to audience members, rather than wasting them on an empty central aisle.

The Lyttelton is also deceptive: that simple, solid-looking stage is actually a jigsaw of lifts, designed to make scene changes swift and nimble, while the proscenium arch can be adjusted to lower the height of the playing space or narrow its width. Unlike the Olivier, where epic work, state-of-the-nation drama and spectacular musicals flourish, the Lyttelton is probably best suited to naturalism and cinematic work: plays and productions that embrace its wide, deep stage and its height, that relish the ability to create framed stage pictures and display intricate sets.

To begin with, there were lengthy debates as to whether the National should have a proscenium arch space at all, with many on the Building Committee arguing that such theatres had had their time and a return to a more open or thrust stage was now the priority. In the end, though, enough committee members were in favour, arguing that the majority of plays written since Shakespeare's time were created with that sort of theatre in mind, that writers such as Coward and Shaw needed a stage suited to their work, that it would support visiting companies accustomed to this more conventional arrangement and that it would be easier to take shows on tour out of it.

Its initial reception, too, was mixed. Some critics welcomed the potential of such a huge, wide stage and the absence of ornamentation. Others complained that it felt impersonal, like a lecture hall. It's true that the sheer size of the stage makes it a challenge to focus the action, while actors can find it hard to make an impact in the expanse.

Getting it right

But the Lyttelton can be dazzling when showcasing a production that suits its vast capacity. When the Quebecois artist Robert Lepage visited in 2001, for instance, he ended *The Far Side of the Moon* with a beautiful image, using the height of the stage to create the effect of him spinning weightlessly in mid-air, like a shirt in a tumble-dryer or a cosmonaut in space. Earlier, in 1986, the Schaubühne Company stunned audiences by erecting what appeared to be a solid ocean liner on the stage for a production of Eugene O'Neill's *The Hairy Ape*, something few theatres would have the space to accommodate.

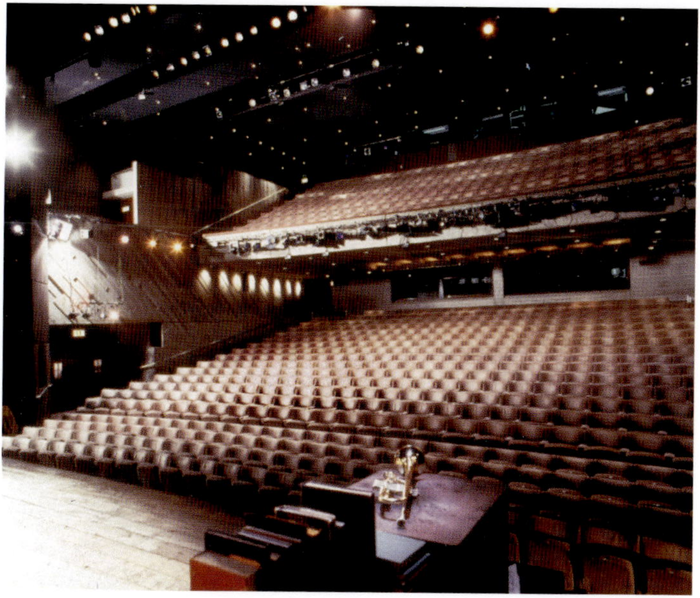

The Lyttelton auditorium

Imaginative directors and designers embrace the scale and technical potential of the stage. Howard Davies, an expert at staging Russian drama, often used the theatre expressively, working with designers to create spectacular, lifelike settings. For his production of *Burnt by the Sun* (2009), set in Russia in 1936, designer Vicki Mortimer filled the stage with an elegant and incredibly realistic wooden summer house with multiple rooms.

Bunny Christie also made excellent use of the space's architectural possibilities when designing Davies' production of *Philistines* (2007). Christie has talked about the need to break up the expanse of the stage, creating corridors, multiple rooms or layers, and using lighting skilfully to help to focus the action and prevent the actors from looking lost. Do that and you make the most of the versatility of the space. Her own detailed set filled the stage with a turn-of-the-century Moscow apartment for Gorky's 1901 play, creating several handsome furnished rooms where the characters read, wrote and argued. Rain ran down the tall windows; the hall recessed back into the depths of the stage; stairs disappeared up towards another storey – you felt you could move in.

Christie's atmospheric design for Bulgakov's *The White Guard* (which she said was inspired by the evocative interiors painted by Danish artist Vilhelm Hammershøi), similarly filled the giant stage with believable buildings. But that show, set in war-torn Kiev in 1918–19, also used the hidden stage mechanics to draw the audience into the mood and meaning of the play. The floor suddenly broke apart so that one apparently solid interior seemed to melt away to be replaced by another. This dizzying visual trick changed the location swiftly and fluently, but also suggested the upheaval and disorientation of conflict and, as Christie described it, the unstoppable 'machinery of war'.

The secret to this manoeuvre is the fact that the floor of the Lyttelton, while appearing solid, is actually made up of hydraulic lifts and the sets are mounted on wagons. Those sets glide onto the stage then the lift is sunk down to bring the wagon flush with the stage floor. That technological wizardry means that changeovers between shows (in which the entire set of one is dismantled and that for another erected) can be executed extremely quickly, taking on average two to four hours (the average is five to eight hours in the Olivier).

The toaster effect

As with the Olivier, the Lyttelton's repertory system demands a huge amount of flexibility, which in turn relies on storage space for sets. There's a 20-metre fly-tower that offers the same cubic capacity above the stage as on it, so sets can be stowed above. Unlike the automated Olivier, the system of ropes and pulleys in the fly-tower is operated, in time honoured fashion, by the crew. Meanwhile the Lyttelton stage itself is in fact L-shaped, with giant shutters hiding an enormous backstage area from the view of the audience. Another set of shutters below and above the front of the stage clamp together like a giant jaw to create the safety curtain. This move is impressive in itself, as anyone who stays in the auditorium during the interval – when the curtain is closed to test it – can tell you.

Another ingenious piece of kit lurks at the front of the stage, in front of the line of the safety curtain. Peer closely and you will see that the floor on this strip of forestage is divided into three sections. These are more elevators, which can be dropped down to create an orchestra pit at the front of the stage. Canny designers have realised that when the lifts are lowered it's also possible to conceal sets in the resulting cavity, which can then be pushed up when needed.

This facility, known in the theatre as 'the toaster effect' because of the way things rise from the narrow rectangular gaps, can also be put to symbolic use. In Dominic Cooke's wonderful 2016 staging of August Wilson's *Ma Rainey's Black Bottom* – a play about racial inequality set within the 1920s American music business – the designer Ultz used these lifts to emphasise the endemic prejudice at work. In Ultz's three-tier set, the white studio bosses were in a closed-off booth high above the stage, the black musicians were in the basement and the studio was sandwiched in between. He achieved this effect by building the 'basement' set on top of the lifts, then sinking the lifts down, so the top of that set was flush with the top of the stage. This meant he could bring the musicians up from the depths to perform scenes set in the rehearsal rooms. It not only made for an efficient transition between scenes, but it also highlighted the inequality that the play was depicting.

Turning heads

The challenge with the Lyttelton is that the circle can't see the stalls, so really you are playing to two audiences. If I am directing a show in there, I put pictures of people's faces high up on the wall in the rehearsal room to remind the actors to get the story up to the circle. But I like the wide-screen of the Lyttelton. Because it's wide, when I direct in there I love to get the actors far apart and make it significant when they get closer together. I like distance between characters: I like more distance on stage than you get in real life. It gives you a fabulous opportunity to get an audience's heads turning as if they were at a tennis match. It's huge – it's an aircraft hangar. It's wonderful.

Patrick Marber, playwright and director

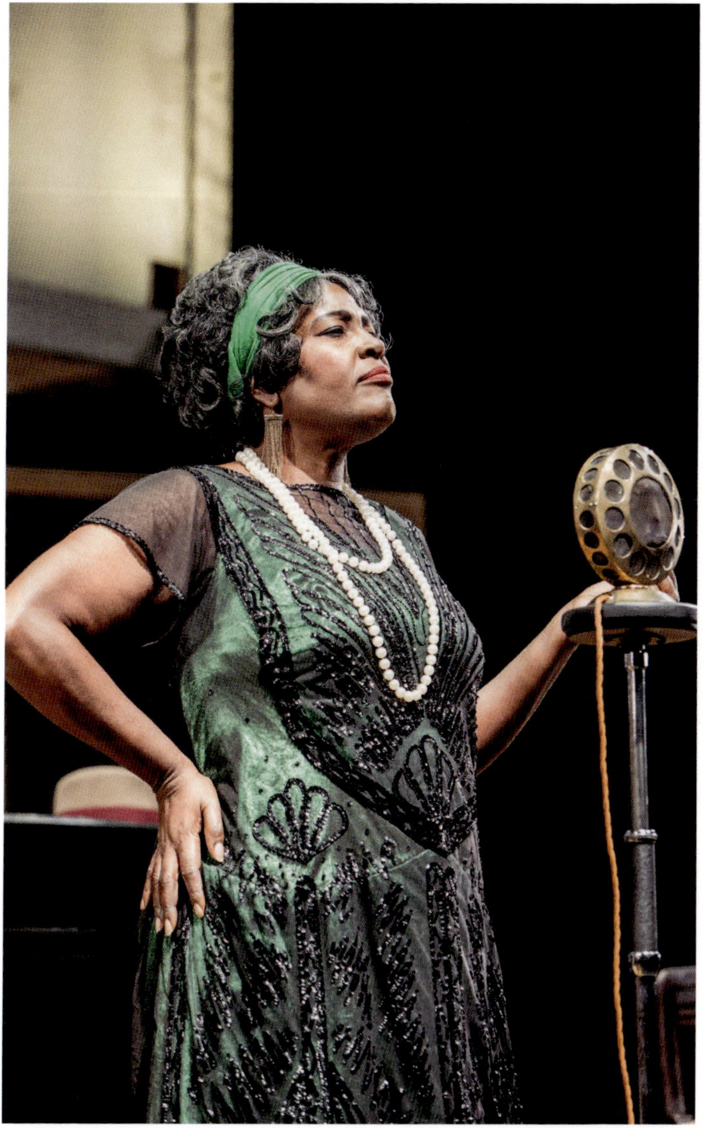

Sharon D Clarke in *Ma Rainey's Black Bottom* (2016)

Enda Walsh's *Misterman* (2012), designed by Jamie Vartan, used the entire scope of the stage, stripping it back and opening up the rear as well. It was, extraordinarily, a one-man show, but actor Cillian Murphy used the huge space, darting around the extremities of a set which filled the whole area with a cavernous, two-tier, disused industrial warehouse. The hit 2018 show *The Lehman Trilogy*, which told the story of the original Lehman brothers behind the bank that so famously went bust in 2008 precipitating the global financial crash, filled the stage with a spinning skeleton of a deserted office.

The Lyttelton has seen its share of triumphs: Richard Bean's riotous farce *One Man, Two Guvnors* premiered here in 2011, with James Corden delighting the audience as a hapless servant who at one point undertakes a physical fight with himself. That hilarious knockabout nonsense suited the picture-frame nature of the stage well. So too did Marianne Elliott's stunning revival of *Angels in America*, in 2017, and a ground-breaking stage adaptation, by the renowned director Ivo van Hove, of the 1976 film *Network*. Van Hove turned the whole space into a huge TV studio and brought audience members on stage to eat at a functioning, on-stage restaurant as part of the action.

But it has also seen its share of calamities, the most notorious being the accident-prone maiden voyage of a cabin cruiser in Alan Ayckbourn's *Way Upstream*. The comedy, premiered in 1982, took place on a river and the plan was to float the boat on a 6,000-gallon tank of water. But the production capsized when the fibreglass tank split, deluging the stage and sub-stage, threatening the main electrical supply for the building and causing thousands of pounds worth of damage, the cancellation of several previews and a flood of satirical headlines in the press (one critic attended the opening night, when it finally arrived, wearing wellington boots).

That problem was ultimately fixed, only for more to surface downstream: the leaks warped the wooden stage floor, costing over £3,000 to repair;

the boat was damaged when it hit the 'river bank' and could no longer brake safely; technicians concealed inside the boat to manoeuvre it started to get motion sickness after hours in the dark; bacteriological tests conducted on the water found it to be alive with nasty little micro-organisms. It did finally open successfully, but the whole production history was certainly a voyage of discovery.

Water also played its part in the arrival on stage of *The History Boys* (2004), Alan Bennett's touching, wise and hilarious comedy about a group of 1980s grammar school teenagers attempting to swot up for university entrance exams. On press night, before the show, someone in the flies lit up a cigarette and the sprinklers sprang into action. The stage was soaked and the lighting system crashed. Alan Bennett remembers encountering a lost fireman negotiating his way around the maze of backstage corridors. Meanwhile, on stage the crew was mopping up and, front of house, an expectant audience was held in the foyer for an hour and plied with free drinks. Eventually the technicians got the lights back on, but the programme controlling the cues had lost its plan for the show. The lighting designer agreed to improvise the lighting, live.

The show went up an hour late and could have gone down in history as one of the theatre's great debacles. In fact, it was a triumph. The audience warmed immediately to Bennett's comic genius and his heartfelt discussion of the purpose of education. In his memoir *Balancing Acts*, then-Director Nicholas Hytner describes it as 'the most euphoric night' he ever spent at the National. The play went on to be one of the most successful shows the theatre has ever staged.

Luke Treadaway in *The Curious Incident of the Dog in the Night-Time* (2012)

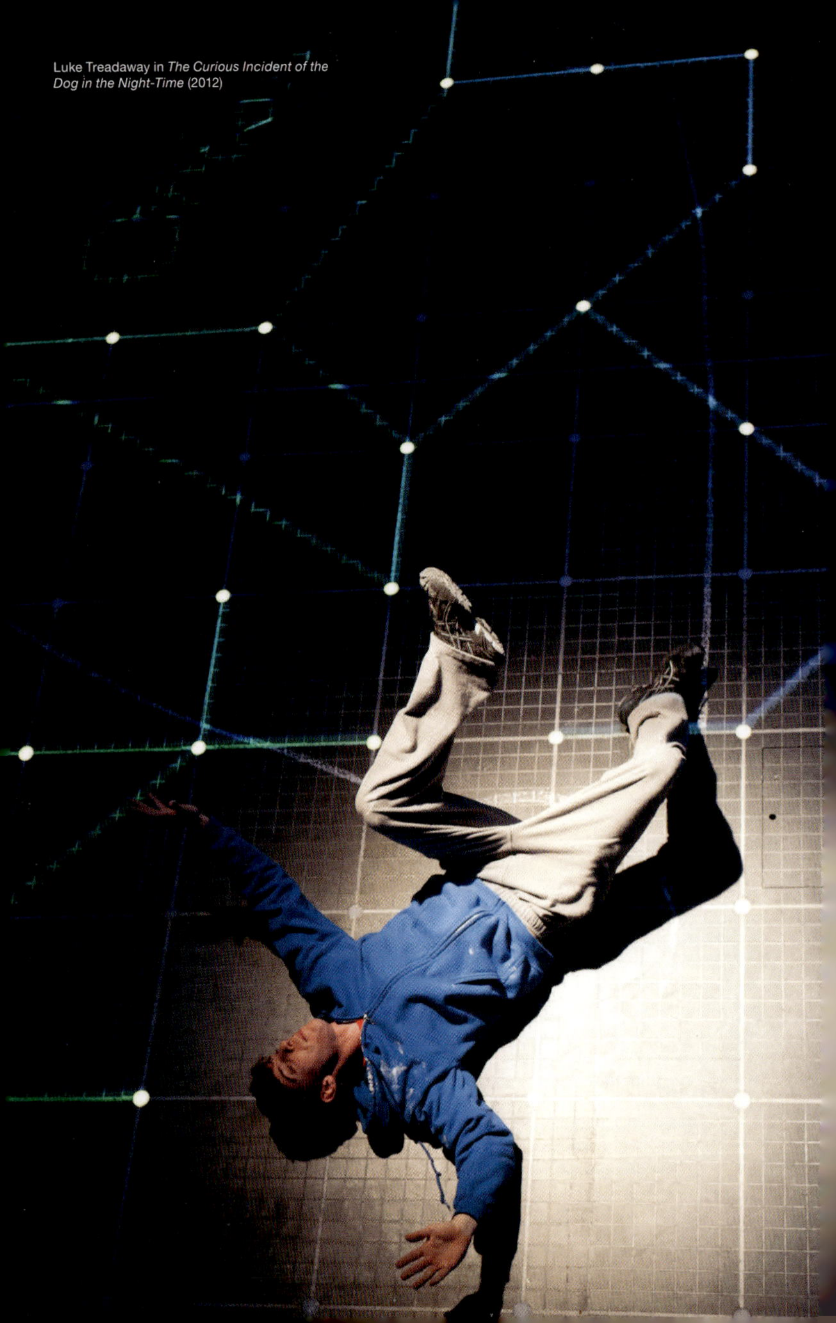

4.
The Dorfman Theatre

The adaptable space

One of the most dramatic performances for the NT's third auditorium did not take place on the stage. In February 1985, the then-Director Peter Hall strode through a group of waiting journalists, leapt onto a coffee table and gave an impromptu speech. He announced that he would be closing the National Theatre's smallest auditorium – then called the Cottesloe – because of squeezed funding. He had warned, he said, that this 'day of reckoning' might come, when just cutting corners throughout the theatre would no longer suffice to make ends meet.

It was a flamboyant, highly risky move and one guaranteed to get attention. Far from reflecting failure on the part of the Cottesloe, Hall's announcement made an impact partly because that space had become so beloved in its opening decade (indeed, it reopened six months later following a one-off grant from the Greater London Council).

The first plans for the National Theatre building included a blueprint for a studio: a smaller space where new and experimental work could first see the light of day – a creative engine room. Mounting costs and shifting priorities put its arrival in jeopardy as the building plans advanced, but, finally, an empty bricked-up space behind the Olivier backstage area was designated and the task of devising a cheap but viable scheme for it passed to theatre building expert, Iain Mackintosh. Mackintosh suggested a mix of contemporary black box studio and courtyard, lined by tiers of galleries resembling those in Georgian playhouses or the inn-yards that once functioned as performance areas.

The resulting theatre, finished in 1977, is a simple but enormously flexible space: a rectangular black box, with three tiers of narrow galleries around three sides, starting at floor level. The moveable seating in the central pit means that it can be snapped into a host of different configurations, with the stage end-on (the most conventional: facing rows of raked seating), traverse (a narrow strip with seats either side), in the round (fringed all round by seats) or promenade (with few or no seats at all in the pit). It's not unusual to arrive at the theatre for a play and find it transformed almost beyond recognition from your last visit. This adaptability, together with the fact that it feels extraordinarily intimate (although it is still significantly larger than many other studio theatres), has made it home to some of the National's most successful and innovative shows.

One of the first to spot the potential in this malleable space was maverick Scottish director Bill Bryden. Peter Hall, fully occupied with getting the rest of the theatre up and running, entrusted the Cottesloe to Bryden in 1977. Bryden took up the challenge with relish, assembling a company around him and soon attracting a devoted audience. Two of that company's productions, in particular, became legendary, using as they did the theatre's full potential to combine the ambitious and the intimate.

The first was *The Passion* (1977), an indoor recreation of one of the York Mystery Plays, a cycle of medieval religious plays telling the story of the Bible, from the creation to the last judgement, and following Jesus from birth to crucifixion. They had once been performed in the streets of York, Chester and Wakefield by craftsmen, using their carts as portable stages, and that combination of a deeply spiritual subject matter with rough-and-ready performance and community spirit appealed enormously to Bryden. He commissioned Yorkshire poet Tony Harrison to rework the texts, while he and his designer William Dudley emptied the entire playing space of seats and suspended makeshift lights (created from dustbins, colanders and miners' lamps) above it. The production drew on traditional working-class culture, folk music and the industrial landscape. The crucifix was made of railway sleepers; God appeared on high, spot-lit in the dark, on the raised platform of a fork-lift truck.

The audience could wander at will, mingling with the actors who were dressed as modern-day tradesmen – they could even take part in the story. They would spend all day seeing the three parts of the cycle and emerge exhilarated by this celebration of the communal nature of theatre. Bryden followed it up with a promenade staging of *Lark Rise to Candleford*, a two-play adaptation of Flora Thompson's touching, semi-autobiographical novels about life in Victorian rural Oxfordshire. The immersive staging allowed audiences to forget the trials of modern life and escape into a simpler agricultural world of harvesting corn and riding in donkey carts.

The theatre has continued to present exciting and pioneering work ever since. It was here that Tony Kushner's epic *Angels in America* had its UK premiere in 1992. Joe Penhall's sharp examination of race, prejudice and mental health *Blue/Orange* made its debut here in 2000. And it was here that Simon Stephens' hugely successful dramatisation of Mark Haddon's *The Curious Incident of the Dog in the Night-Time* was first performed. The drama's focus was Christopher, a teenager with a brilliant mathematical brain and some behavioural difficulties. On stage, designer Bunny Christie, lighting designer Paule Constable and video designer Finn Ross drew audiences into Christopher's mind, using projections to surround them with the world as he saw it, communicating experiences such as the terror of travelling on the underground or the exhilaration of solving a complex maths problem.

In *London Road* (2011), an extraordinary verbatim piece based on a community's experience of living with a serial killer in their midst, writer Alecky Blythe and composer Adam Cork boldly and brilliantly took the form of the musical in a new direction. All of these shows, which made the most of the intimacy of the smaller auditorium, have since gone on to success on a much larger scale – *Curious Incident*, in particular, became a long-running West End hit and also transferred to Broadway.

It's a space that suits innovation and is dedicated to new work. It's here that Francis Turnly's *The Great Wave* premiered in 2018, bringing a cast entirely of East Asian origin to an NT stage for the first time, and also Inua Ellams' *Barber Shop Chronicles* (2017): a wonderful, vivacious piece, set in barber shops around the world, which explored the experience of being a black man.

Anything is possible

When Indhu Rubasingham telephoned me with the news that the National Theatre was going to produce my play *The Great Wave* and that she would be directing, it took a while to sink in. I wasn't able to sleep for days, worrying about the length of the playscript and about how we could create the sea on stage. Over the course of a year, I had the opportunity to workshop the play at the National's New Work department and managed to cut it down from 300 to 120 pages. Watching the first preview was nerve-racking but when I saw how a sense of the sea had been created through Oliver Fenwick's lighting, Alex Caplen's sound design and Luke Halls' stunning projections I knew we had something special and became excited to write more plays, knowing anything I could imagine was possible.

— Francis Turnly, playwright

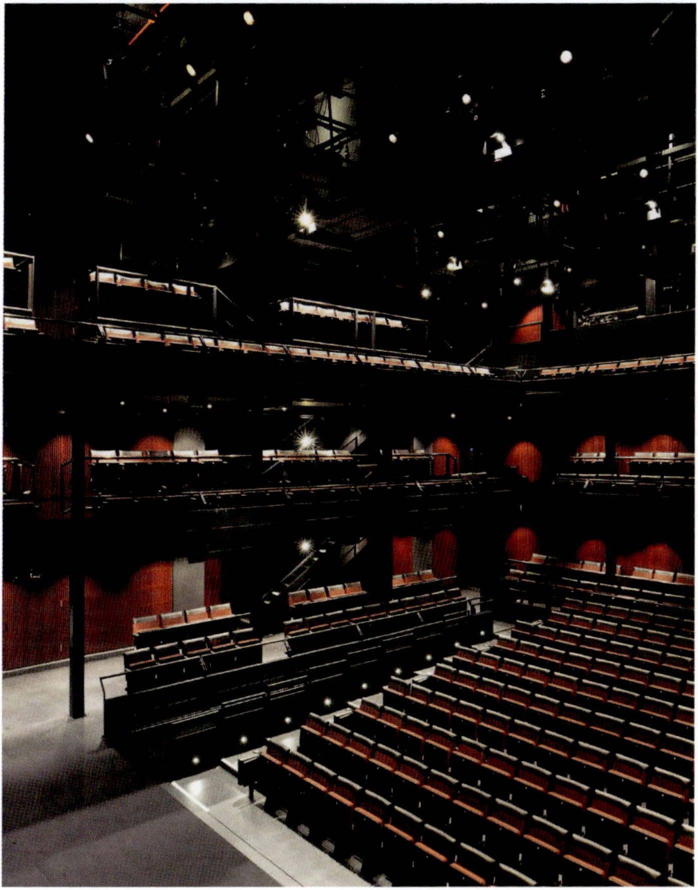

The Dorfman auditorium

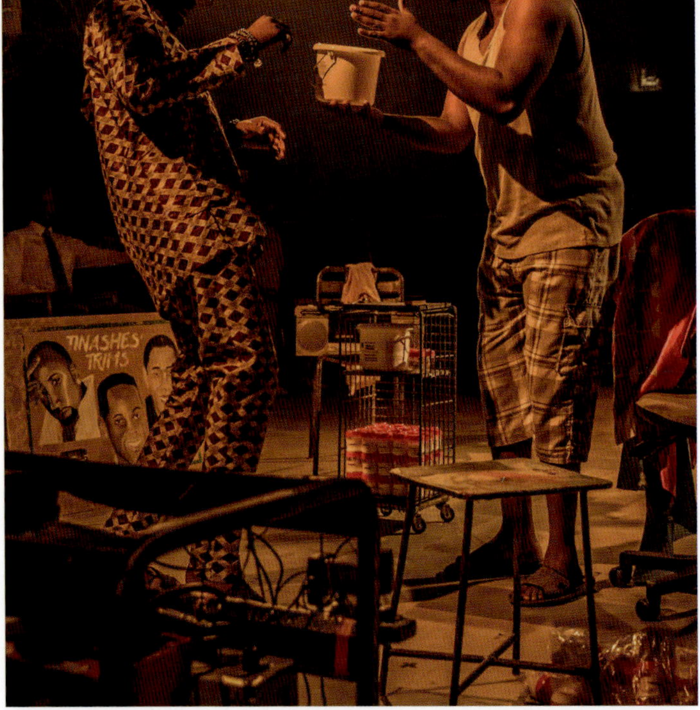

Sule Rimi and Hammed Animashaun in *Barber Shop Chronicles* (2017)

A facelift

But the very flexibility that made the Cottesloe so attractive was laborious to achieve, with changes of seating configuration being both laborious and time-consuming. The limited number of total seats was a financial constraint; the poor air conditioning was a discomfort; the absence of backstage facilities was a limit; the tiny foyer was a headache before shows and during intervals, as crowds struggled past one another to access the bar, toilets, cloakrooms and auditorium. Meanwhile the theatre's location, at the back of the building with a separate entrance barely visible from the river and approached via a walk past the bins, meant that it felt rather tacked on and forgotten.

The NT Future refurbishment tackled many of these issues. The Cottesloe got a facelift, a host of new, comfort-enhancing features and many technical improvements. It was also given a new name: it is now called the Dorfman Theatre, after Lloyd Dorfman, the philanthropist whose company Travelex sponsored the theatre's Travelex cheap ticket system and who pledged £10 million to NT Future, helping it get off the ground.

The theatre can now hold an audience of up to 450 – judicious repositioning of the control room and the staircases has increased seating capacity as well as improving sight-lines. Theatre design consultants Charcoalblue worked on improving the seating technology, adding jump-seats at the end of the rows that can be folded out for use and folded away again for storage. They also introduced a hydraulic system, which means that the seats can be manoeuvred into new positions, folded into the floor or the rake altered from steep to shallow, all by remote control. Now just four technicians can take the seating configuration from a flat floor to a steeply raked auditorium in just 45 minutes. The air conditioning was rerouted, so that it would not be compromised by variations in the playing space.

The Dorfman reopened in party mood in 2014 with *Here Lies Love*, an immersive show that both celebrated its new lease of life and harked back to those early successes of *The Mysteries* and *Lark Rise to Candleford*. For this exuberant disco-musical (by David Byrne and DJ Fatboy Slim) about Imelda Marcos, the whole auditorium was transformed into a pulsating nightclub, complete with glitter-ball and dazzling light show, the audience on the dance floor playing first clubbers then crowds.

The theatre still retains some of its original backstage limitations. Its genesis as an empty room means that not only does it have no fly-tower, there is also no backstage, side-stage, under-stage, lift nor any other nook or cranny where sets or props can be stored. In addition, it has only one door out from the stage level, so everything – sets, furniture, props – has to go in and out through that door. Short of knocking the theatre down and starting again, such features are impossible to address – and so simple and spare often works best in here. In fact, you could say that where the Olivier rewards boldness and the Lyttleton encourages veracity, the more intimate, versatile Dorfman Theatre inspires ingenuity – on the part of set designers and directors alike.

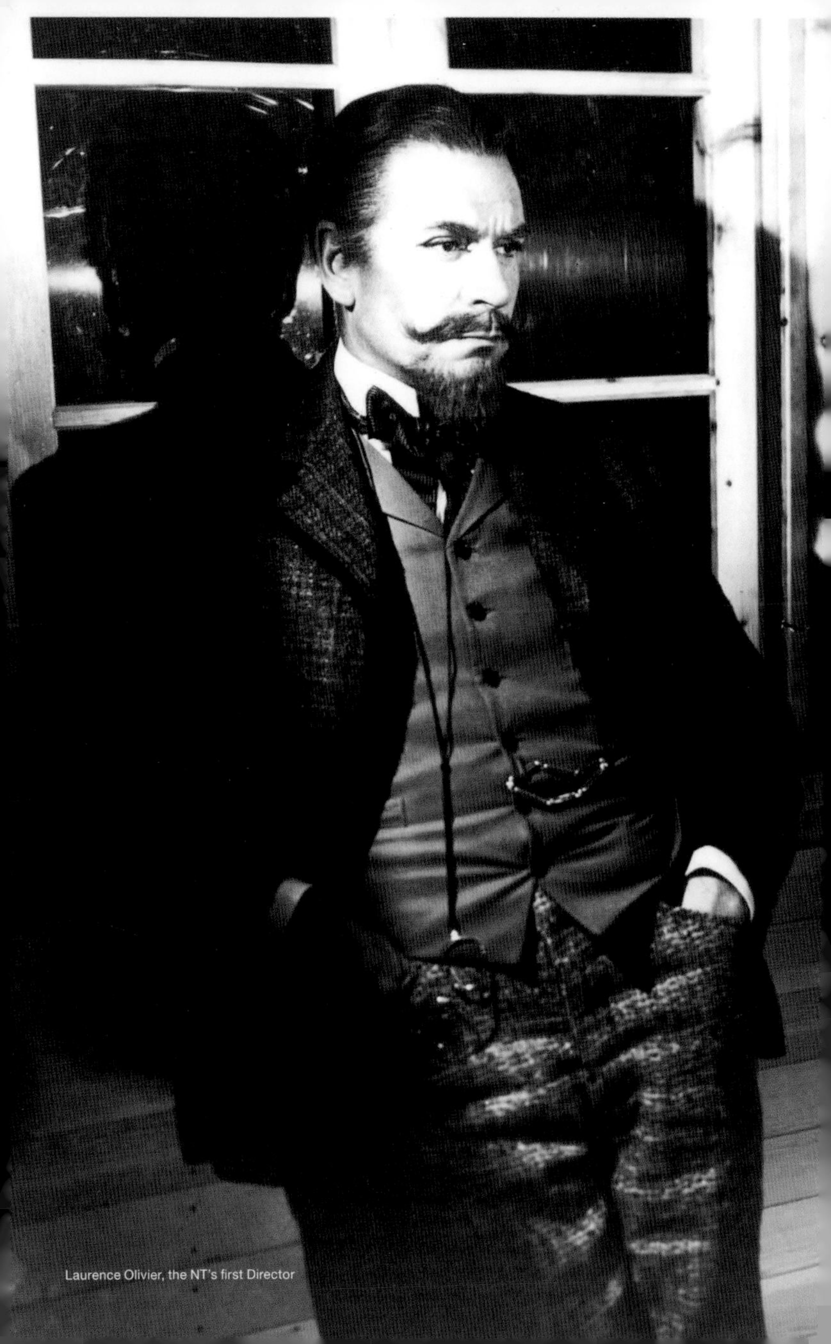

Laurence Olivier, the NT's first Director

6.
The Directors

1. Laurence Olivier 1963–1973

When Laurence Olivier was appointed first Director of the National Theatre, even he admitted how daunting the prospect was. 'I don't think I'm really the right man for the job, but I can't think of anyone better,' he said.

It was certainly true that, with his fame and charisma, he was one of very few people who could have pulled off the role of figurehead for the fledgling theatre. Aged 55 at the time of his appointment, he was a household name: one of the greatest actors of his generation – an electric presence on stage and a glamorous, intensely charming man off stage. He had been knighted in 1947. He had experience not just as an actor, but also as a director, a manager and an impresario. In the public consciousness he was associated with a stirring wartime film performance of Shakespeare's Henry V – no bad thing if you want to rouse the nation to get behind your project – and he arrived at the National fresh from opening the brand new Chichester Festival Theatre.

His task was to establish the ethos and direction of the National Theatre, while working in its temporary home at the Old Vic, and, at the same time, appoint an architect to design a permanent, purpose-built home. It was certainly a challenge and Olivier gave up alcohol for a year to be fitter for the job.

While keeping one foot firmly in tradition, Olivier also gathered into the company younger, more radical talents, such as directors John Dexter and William Gaskill from London's Royal Court Theatre. One particularly smart move was to bring Kenneth Tynan, the fierce and outspoken critic, into the fold as dramaturg (Olivier later admitted that his wife, Joan Plowright, advised him that it would be better to have Tynan inside the tent, rather than outside). And he made the venue an actors' theatre, assembling a 50-strong company, among them Michael Redgrave, Cyril Cusack, Maggie Smith, Billie Whitelaw, Frank Finlay, Derek Jacobi, Robert Stephens and Michael Gambon. He ruffled feathers, however, by not including some of the luminaries of his own generation and by opening the theatre with a guest star – Peter O'Toole – as Hamlet.

Olivier's first season in 1963 launched with that *Hamlet*, directed by him, and included a production of *Othello*, in which he played the lead role. By the following year, the company had introduced world premieres alongside classic revivals, with Peter Shaffer's *The Royal Hunt of the Sun* being the first new play. It had also begun the practice both of touring the country and of inviting visiting foreign companies to showcase their work (starting with *Hamlet* from the Italian Compagnia Proclemer-Albertazzi). The famous Italian director Franco Zeffirelli visited to stage *Much Ado About Nothing* (1965). Olivier continued to direct and act in shows regularly – his last stage performance would be in Trevor Griffiths' *The Party* in 1973 – and to be intimately involved with the running of the theatre: actor Derek Jacobi recalled in a BBC *Arena* interview, that even when ill in hospital with prostate cancer, Olivier would phone through from the ward. He could be both convivial and imposing: Maggie Smith would later recall how intimidating she found him when she was a young actress.

By the end of his tenure, Olivier had established the National Theatre as a prestigious and influential actor-led company and he had, after much wrangling both inside the Building Committee and outside in the broader political sphere, been able to agree a design for the new building on the South Bank and perform the 'topping out' ceremony in 1973. But the matter of who would succeed him was clumsily handled. The board began looking for a replacement and settled on Peter Hall, the dynamic young director who had founded the Royal Shakespeare Company. Olivier was taken aback – he regarded Hall as a friendly rival – and felt that he had been left out of the process. He appeared only once at the new National Theatre, on the stage named after him, to deliver a speech on the official opening night in 1976. But he would go on to praise Peter Hall, saying: 'If I could claim any responsibility for putting the theatre up, he can claim for getting people into it.'

2. Peter Hall 1973–1988

There is an image of Laurence Olivier and Peter Hall standing side by side at around the time of Hall's succession to the post of Director. In many ways it seems to crystallise the differences in style between the two men. Olivier is smart but formal in a suit and tie; Hall wears a black polo-neck sweater and a black leather jacket. It was a generational shift, but also a shift of emphasis: Olivier came from the older generation of actor-managers, while Hall represented a move into what was loosely called 'directors' theatre'. A man of phenomenal energy, charisma and tenacity, Hall had staged the English premiere of Samuel Beckett's *Waiting for Godot* when in his mid 20s, had founded the Royal Shakespeare Company when he was just 29 and had pioneered a fresh approach to Shakespearean text.

His job upon becoming Director was daunting. The construction of the new NT building was underway, but subject to endless delays and setbacks: he had to cancel several productions and, in the end, simply moved into the unfinished structure once one auditorium (the Lyttelton) was complete. The company rehearsed in what was still, in many places, a building site. 'The noise of banging and hammering all over the building made it impossible to concentrate,' he wrote in his diary, after one particularly trying afternoon rehearsal.

Even once the building finally opened fully, in 1976, the problems continued: industrial relations across the country were in turmoil and a wave of strikes hit the National Theatre. 'I had to learn about industrial relations on a sort of crash course,' Hall would say later in a television interview. He was faced with financial worries, negative press and, during the 1980s, a Conservative government set on cutting the arts budget.

Hall, like Olivier, opened the new chapter in the National's existence by staging *Hamlet* – the first production on the Lyttelton stage. Unlike Olivier, however, he had to fill not one theatre, but three, with a wide-ranging repertoire. He went on to direct and oversee some ground-breaking pieces of work: among them a landmark, masked production of the ancient Greek tragedy *The Oresteia* on the Olivier stage (1981), a seminal *Antony and Cleopatra*, with Anthony Hopkins and Judi Dench as the tragic lovers (1987) and a stinging, and immensely topical political drama about newspaper ownership, *Pravda* (1985), by Howard Brenton and David Hare. Hall's time in charge also saw the premiere of *Amadeus* by Peter Shaffer (1979), the trauma around Brenton's controversial *Romans in Britain* (1980), and the first musical at the National – *Guys and Dolls* (1982).

Hall was knighted in 1977. When he stood down as Director in 1988, he and the building had weathered an immensely turbulent period in British politics, and the National had become a permanent fixture with an international reputation. He would continue to be a globally renowned director and a galvanising force in British theatre. He returned to the National to stage Shakespeare's *Twelfth Night* in 2011 with his daughter Rebecca as Viola.

3. Richard Eyre 1988–1997

The director who had staged *Guys and Dolls* at the National in 1982, using the Olivier theatre with such aplomb and establishing a precedent for dazzling productions of musicals at the theatre, was Richard Eyre. He would go on to become, in 1988, the NT's third Director. Eyre had already run Nottingham Playhouse, where he had staged many new plays, and had produced the contemporary drama programme *Play for Today* for the BBC. He brought that appetite for bold, topical and large-scale new work to the National, cementing the principle that the theatre could and should act as a public forum on occasions: a place to address and contemplate the big issues of the day.

'It's impossible to be in that office and not feel you have a responsibility to reflect the feeling of the nation,' he told a BBC *Arena* programme marking the NT's 50th birthday. 'And that's the job. That's what the theatre exists to do.'

Most famously, Eyre commissioned and directed David Hare's trilogy about major British institutions: *Racing Demon* (the Church of England), *Murmuring Judges* (the legal system) and *The Absence of War* (politics). These were plays that spoke directly to audiences about current affairs: Eyre staged all three in one day on the Olivier stage in 1993, creating a palpable sense of excitement and reminding audiences of how potent live contemporary theatre could be.

A more reticent man than his predecessor, Eyre confessed in his published diaries how hard the job of running the National had been and the doubts and difficulties he had endured. There certainly were low spots, such as the poorly received and poorly attended farce *Johnny on a Spot* (1994), and traumas, such as Daniel Day-Lewis walking out of a production of *Hamlet* (1989) mid-way through a performance (he has not acted on stage since).

But Eyre's period at the helm of the National was immensely successful and pushed forward the theatre's identity. There were some terrific new plays: Tony Kushner's epic *Angels in America* (1992), talking openly about the AIDS crisis and the political reaction to it; Alan Bennett's *A Question of Attribution* (1988) about Anthony Blunt, who was both a spy and personal art adviser to the Queen, and his poignant piece *The Madness of George III* (1991); Jim Cartwright's *The Rise and Fall of Little Voice* (1992); the dazzling and funny *Arcadia* (1993) by Tom Stoppard. Eyre championed new writers, such as Patrick Marber with *Dealer's Choice* (1995) and *Closer* (1997), and encouraged a new generation of directors such as Nicholas Hytner, Katie Mitchell, Deborah Warner, Simon McBurney and Declan Donnellan. There were also revivals that reinvigorated classic plays: Ian Holm as a devastating King Lear (1997),

Ian McKellen as a chilling Richard III in an alternative, fascist 1930s Britain (1992) and an expressionist production of JB Priestley's *An Inspector Calls* from Stephen Daldry (1992). The theatre also toured more than ever before (including the first-ever visit by a British theatre company to Lithuania) and worked on co-productions with companies around the country.

Looking back at his time at the helm of the National, Eyre recalled one of the best parts of the job as being what he identified as 'the opposite of Schadenfreude': the joy in being able to give a platform to other artists and watch them flourish. He was knighted in 1997, just a few months before he stepped down to hand over the reins to his successor.

4. Trevor Nunn 1997–2003

When Eyre stood down as Director, it was widely supposed that a rising young director might take his place: Stephen Daldry, say, or Sam Mendes (both in their 30s) or Nicholas Hytner (who would eventually become Director, some six years later). But in the end the job went to a man in his 50s with a proven track record.

That man was Trevor Nunn, who had, at age 27, succeeded Peter Hall as artistic director of the RSC. Nunn arrived with a reputation for combining brilliant work on Shakespeare – such as his intense, claustrophobic 1976 production of *Macbeth*, starring Judi Dench and Ian McKellen – with an eye for the epic and the popular. He had premiered the RSC's nine-hour staging of Dickens' novel *Nicholas Nickleby*; more famously still he had also staged the literary musicals *Cats* (based on *Old Possum's Book of Practical Cats* by TS Eliot), *Les Misérables* (based on the Victor Hugo novel) and the roller-skating extravaganza *Starlight Express* – all of which had become colossal hits. He was sanguine both at the time of his appointment and later about the role that he might be expected to play at the National at a time when government funding was at a standstill. 'They [the National Theatre] wanted a period of consolidation,' he would later say in a BBC interview. 'I knew that was what was expected of me.'

Nunn brought in many popular musicals – *Oklahoma* (1998), *South Pacific* (2001), *Anything Goes* (2002) and *My Fair Lady* (2001) – drawing criticism from those who felt that the National should be staging more challenging fare. Nunn's contention was always that the line drawn between high art and show-business was a fairly arbitrary one and that Shakespeare himself would place searing tragedy and knockabout comedy side by side in one play (the porter scene in *Macbeth* for instance).

But he also staged 35 new plays, including Michael Frayn's dazzling *Copenhagen* (1998); Joe Penhall's clever and challenging *Blue/Orange* (2000); Mark Ravenhill's *Mother Clap's Molly House* (2001); a technically demanding pair of plays by Alan Ayckbourn – *House* and *Garden* (1999) – that necessitated a cast of actors sprinting from one stage to another throughout the evening; plus work from Roy Williams, Richard Bean and Tanika Gupta. And he mounted a season called 'Transformation', in a new 100-seat theatre at the top of the building, to allow more experimental drama to be staged by emerging young talents and to introduce new audiences to new work at new prices. He was knighted in 2002.

5. Nicholas Hytner 2003–2015

'We want to make art, we know we're in show-business,' wrote Nicholas Hytner in his memoir *Balancing Acts*, looking back on his time as Director and neatly summing up the many paradoxes that faced him and all of his predecessors in running this enormous and ambitious playhouse. That keen understanding fuelled Hytner's enormously successful period in charge, together with his aspiration that 'the National Theatre should examine the constituent parts of its title, and explore both the state of the nation and the boundaries of the theatre.'

Under Hytner, the NT would work hard to fulfil those aims. He was determined to open the theatre up further, to pull new work out of small studio theatres and onto the big stages and to galvanise and attract new audiences both within the building itself and further afield. Soon after he arrived, the theatre secured the Travelex sponsorship that would underwrite cheap tickets and encourage younger and less affluent theatre-goers to attend: throughout the Travelex £10 Season two-thirds of tickets in the Olivier would be pegged at £10. Hytner would go on to launch National Theatre Live – the live transmission of productions to cinemas worldwide for audiences unable to attend the shows in person – and to build on the practices of touring and West End transfers. The development of National Theatre Productions, a team to oversee this arm of NT work, also ensured that the theatre retained the financial responsibility for such endeavours and so was able to recycle any profits back into the system to sustain future work.

Hytner had a very close working partnership with his Executive Director, Nick Starr. They worked together on many ambitious projects, including the massive NT Future transformation of the building, which opened up its riverfront view, improved the foyer spaces, refurbished the Dorfman Theatre, created a new education space, and added the Max Rayne Centre to house the workshops. When Hytner left the National in 2015, the theatre both looked and felt more inclusive and open.

He opened with a statement of intent. One of the earliest shows was *Jerry Springer: The Opera*, a flamboyantly foul-mouthed musical based on the TV chat show and asking big questions, beneath all the satire, about the moral responsibility of television. And the first show Hytner himself directed was a Shakespeare, but not *Hamlet*, as Olivier and Hall had chosen. Instead he staged a vibrant and timely *Henry V*: a modern-dress production of a play about the politics of going to war, mounted against the backdrop of unease about the Iraq War and starring a black British actor – Adrian Lester – as the king. It received great reviews, expressed Hytner's conviction that Shakespeare is 'the new century's sharpest political commentator' and put down a marker about the theatre's intentions regarding improving representation on stage.

Looking back on his time, Hytner admitted there had been mistakes – not enough plays, initially, by female writers, for instance (in 2008, Rebecca Lenkiewicz's *Her Naked Skin* was the first play ever by a female writer to be staged in the Olivier). During the final two years of Hytner's tenure there were more new works by women than by men but, by his own admission, 'it took too long'.

But Hytner staged, and programmed, some of the theatre's most successful shows to date: Alan Bennett's poignant comedy *The History Boys* (2004); Richard Bean's deliriously funny adaptation of a Goldoni farce *The Servant of Two Masters*, retitled *One Man, Two Guvnors* (2011); David Hare's probing *Stuff Happens* (2004), which built on that tradition of mounting bitingly topical drama that addressed the big issues of the day; *This House* (2012), James Graham's hilarious comedy about 1970s politics; *The Curious Incident of the Dog in the Night-Time* (2012), adapted by Simon Stephens from the moving novel by Mark Haddon; and, above all, *War Horse* (2007), a wartime story starring a non-speaking equine puppet in the lead that would go on to be a worldwide hit. He left the National Theatre on a high.

6. Rufus Norris 2015–present

Rufus Norris has run the National Theatre since 2015, alongside Executive Director Lisa Burger. While all previous Directors have worked closely with their Executive Directors, Norris and Burger are joint CEOs, sharing responsibility for the vision, running and direction of the theatre, and jointly overseeing the increasingly ambitious spectrum of work taking place in the building and beyond. Before his appointment as Director, Norris had frequently directed at the National and was an AssociateDirector, while Burger had been heavily involved in many of the major projects of the previous decade as Chief Operating Officer.

As with Hytner, the first production Norris directed was a statement of intent. *Everyman* was a bold adaptation by poet laureate Carol Ann Duffy of the 15th-century morality tale, with BAFTA-winning actor Chiwetel Ejiofor playing the eponymous everyman. It considered modern materialism and impending climate disaster, taking place on set designer Ian MacNeil's contemporary neon landscape. The production brought together many of the elements that would define the aim of the NT under Norris: to make theatre for everyone. 'We are being very active in how we think about that *everyone*,' said Burger in a 2019 interview, 'in terms of the programme of work, the people who are making that programme, and the staff who are facilitating that work and helping to take it out beyond this building'.

Contemporary resonance combined with a progressive approach to on-stage representation have become hallmarks of Norris' artistic projects as Director. In the wake of the EU referendum, he commissioned a project collecting reflections from people right across the UK, which would later become the verbatim production *My Country; a work in progress.* In 2019, Norris directed *Small Island*, an adaptation of Andrea Levy's novel set in Jamaica and London leading up to the arrival of *HMT Empire Windrush*.

'It's absolutely imperative that the whole country feels that the arts are for them,' Norris told the *Financial Times*, ahead of the opening of *Small Island*: 'That's why I get so passionate about arts in education and why we're increasing our work outside London, trying to earn the "national" part of our title more ... At the end of this stewardship, I would love to be able to look at the work that is going on and go: that is "national".'

More work has toured the UK than ever before, including *Jane Eyre*, *Barber Shop Chronicles*, *A Taste of Honey*, and a version of Marianne Elliott's production of *The Curious Incident of the Dog in the Night-Time* specially adapted to tour into schools. As part of the original team who created the international broadcast programme National Theatre Live in 2009 Burger has overseen its expansion to 2,500 cinemas in 65 countries.

Meanwhile, the emphasis has continued to shift towards projects that show children, young people and adults across the country that theatre is for them – whether as audiences, creators, writers or technicians. The Learning department has continued to grow, aiming to create opportunities to for children and young people, and support for teachers. The most prominent of these is the participatory theatre programme, Public Acts. The first year of Public Acts culminated in a production of *Pericles* in the Olivier Theatre, featuring 123 performers from community groups who had little or no prior experience of theatre, plus 99 people from local performance groups. The result was a celebration of theatre, of community and of what it feels like to belong.

Not everything has worked, of course: there have been several large-scale shows that have misfired and others that divided audience opinion. There have also been heated debates about the best way to achieve the company's commitment to increased equality and representation.

Perhaps the defining feature of the Norris and Burger's era to date has been breadth of programming. Landmark productions of modern classics, such as Tony Kushner's *Angels in America* and Stephen Sondheim's *Follies*, have rubbed shoulders with plays by Shakespeare and Chekhov, while new writing has featured heavily in the programming for all three theatres. One of Norris' first decisions as Director was to create the New Work department, bringing together the devising and workshop slate of the Studio with the script commissioning and development focus of the Literary department. Among several recent West End transfers of plays, including *Consent* (2017) by Nina Raine and *Home, I'm Darling* (2018) by Laura Wade, Natasha Gordon's debut play *Nine Night* (2018) stands out. A story about the peculiarities of family, both raucously funny and sad by equal measure, *Nine Night*'s transfer to Trafalgar Studios also represented a real milestone for diversity, becoming the first play by a Black British female playwright to be staged in the West End.

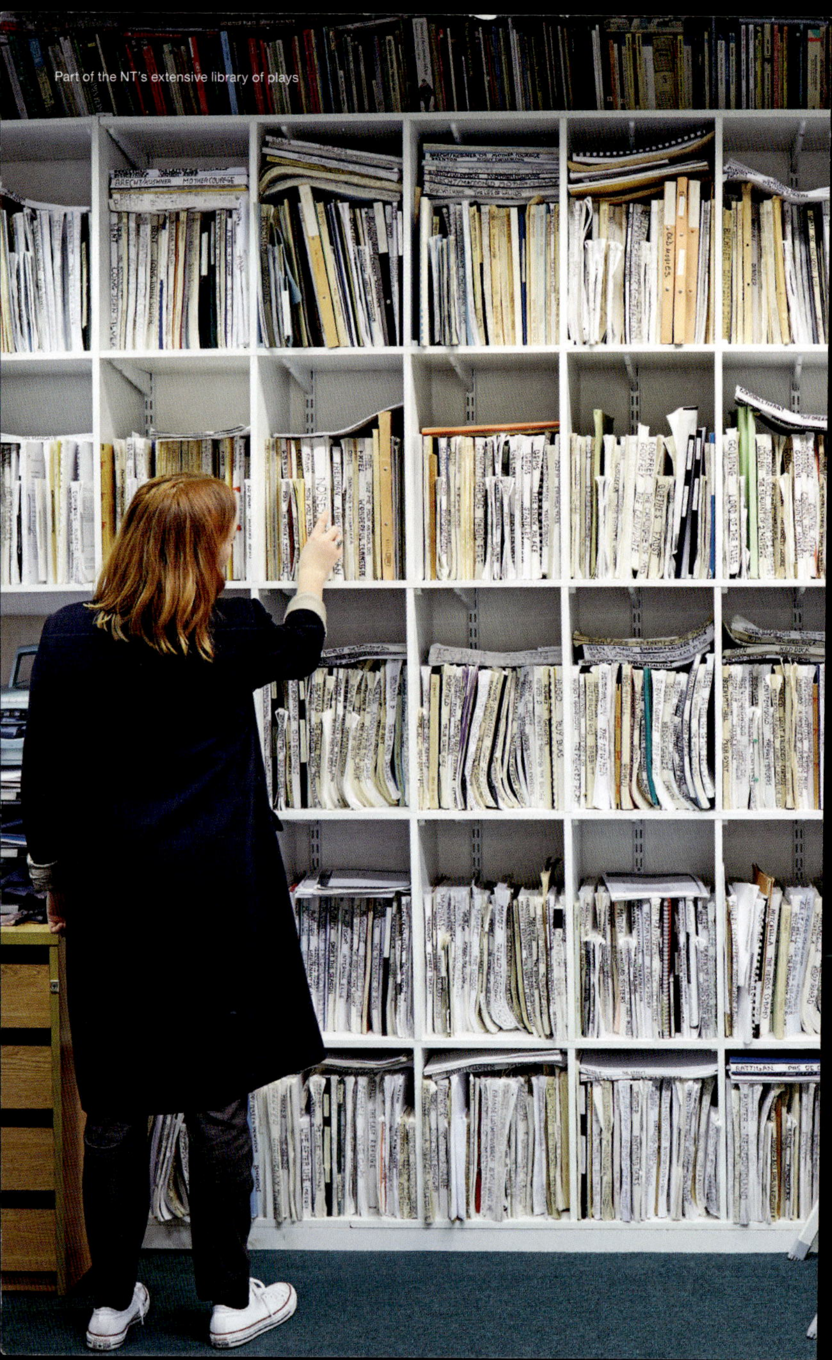

Part of the NT's extensive library of plays

7.
The Plays

A delicate balance

No matter how chilled the wine, how tasty the cakes or how soft the seating, in the end the National Theatre stands or falls on one thing: the work on stage. To paraphrase Hamlet, the plays are the thing: they are at the heart of everything the theatre stands for. So which plays should they be?

That debate has raged since the theatre company first blinked its way into the light in 1963. It's a challenge that faces every artistic director across the globe, but it is particularly acute at the NT, because of the theatre's status as a flagship for the art form and because it has not one, but three theatres to programme, year-round, in a constantly rolling repertory system. The theatre mounts somewhere between 20 and 25 plays a year (and that is before you include co-productions, touring work and transfers). Programming the National is, in creative terms, a little like refuelling a jet in mid-air – you can't stop, you've got to keep airborne and you've got to keep the energy coming. Ben Power, former Deputy Artistic Director, sums up some of the challenges:

'The NT is meant to deliver the best new work,' he explains. 'It's also meant to deliver canonical revivals at a level of excellence that nowhere else can match. There's a responsibility towards internationalism, there's a responsibility towards national remit and voices from across the country – plus we have a progressive and inclusive set of targets in terms of exactly who's telling the stories on stage.

'Also, because we have three theatres and because they are playing in repertoire, you want to have a range of forms and styles and types of experience. If at one moment you had three broad comedies playing in all three theatres, or three Shakespearean tragedies, that wouldn't be a balanced repertoire ... It's about constantly offering plurality and considering what a "theatre for everyone" means. And that's really difficult because you're trying to be all things to all people.'

It's not just about internal balance either: the National doesn't really want to be doing a rare Ibsen revival if every other theatre in London is doing a rare Ibsen revival at the same time. And if the NT does stage a rare Ibsen revival, it needs to have something of substance to say to a modern-day audience. Often, the theatre will look for a fresh twist to a well-known play by having a contemporary writer craft a new adaptation – such as Polly Stenham's 2018 *Julie* (based on Strindberg's *Miss Julie*); Patrick Marber's version of Ibsen's *Hedda Gabler* in 2016 or Carol Ann Duffy's 2015 update of *Everyman*.

But a vital part of the NT repertoire is new work. In 1964 the NT staged its first piece of new work, Peter Shaffer's ambitious *The Royal Hunt of the Sun,* and famous premieres have included Harold Pinter's *No Man's Land*, Tom Stoppard's *Arcadia*, Michael Frayn's *Copenhagen*, Alan Bennett's *The History Boys* and *Pravda* by Howard Brenton and David Hare. More recently around half (10–15) of the plays produced each year have been new work, including the entire Dorfman programme (7–8 plays).

Commissioning original new work is a delicate task. There's a responsibility to be representative across gender, ethnicity and subject matter and there is also a duty of care towards the artists themselves. Getting a new play staged at the National Theatre is a great platform for a playwright – but it can also be enormously exposing. If your play nose-dives, it does so in a very high-profile space and the theatre's stages, particularly the Lyttelton and the Olivier, are challenging to write for. No other theatre in the UK hosting new writing remotely resembles the Olivier or matches it for scale. It's a place that seats over a thousand people and suits epic work that combines human dilemmas with an element of rhetorical flourish. But how does a modern playwright compose such work without sounding awkward or self-conscious?

'There is nowhere where you are going to have an experience anything like writing for the Olivier,' says Power. 'Just the technical skill you need: the knowledge of how long it takes for somebody entering the Olivier stage to be able to speak, and how you have to construct a scene in order to manage that – let alone the ideas, the idiom, the form that can speak to that room. It requires poetry. There are not many other places where you would do that. You have to evolve the muscle of writing for them.'

The engine room

Much of the work preparing new writing is done at the National Theatre Studio. This modest building sits a few streets away from the National Theatre (and just along the road from the company's initial home, the Old Vic). It looks a bit like an old post office sorting depot or a functional local government building. You could easily walk right past it. But this unassuming office block is, in fact, a lively creative laboratory, vital to the work of the theatre.

Founded in 1984, by the playwright and director Peter Gill, the NT Studio is the engine room of the theatre: an essential haven for artists looking to write, experiment and try things out. It is home to the New Work department, which fuses the script-focused development of a literary department with physical devising, workshopping and experimentation. Here a new play might be written or have its first rehearsed reading, a fresh take on a classic drama might be developed and tried out, or a risky project – such as *War Horse* or *London Road* – might get its first outing.

The Studio offers artists a pressure-free environment in which to test out ideas. Artists can hold readings, workshop plays, explore ideas or perhaps work with actors to develop a script to the scale demanded by the Olivier. In one year as many as 1,000 artists might work here and at any one time the New Work department might have up to 70 plays on commission and another 200 projects under discussion. They also receive around 1,500 unsolicited scripts a year, every one of which is read by a panel, some of which go on to be produced.

'We have a team of readers who read all the submissions,' says Emily McLaughlin, Head of New Work. 'They are trusted gatekeepers. They read everything and then meet to discuss what they've read. Then things get escalated up so we will read what they're recommending. We read, we cover, we assess – we are a kind of a portal for most artists to approach the NT with what it is they want to do and to be considered.'

The building has the quiet hum you'd expect of a creative hub. On the third floor are writers' rooms where playwrights can work on scripts. The Studio can house up to eight writers at a time this way, offering invaluable space to focus on a piece of work while at the same time giving them access to other writers – including the Writer in Residence, who acts as a mentor – and to the New Work department to discuss ideas or try them out with actors. Every writer on attachment gets paid the same rate, which is £90 per day (at the time of writing).

The kind of writers who may be offered an attachment vary. Often they are playwrights whose work the dramaturgs at the Studio find interesting, but who are perhaps not quite ready for a commission. At other times an attachment will come out of a workshop: if a workshop has happened and the feeling is that the script needs some specific work, the writer can be given space and support to do that.

'They're free to come and go. It's not school, we're not taking a register every morning,' explains New Work Administrator Sarah Clarke. 'We don't expect homework handed in and we don't expect a play at the end of it – though it is lovely if we get one. If something comes out of it we get first refusal. But if it's not quite right for us, it can go elsewhere: as the National Theatre part of our remit is keeping the theatrical eco-system healthy.'

Different writers use the space in different ways. Some are very quiet and focused; others like to debate and discuss with other dramatists and get plenty of input on what they are writing. Some will work methodically from nine to five: one writer handed in his phone and computer at the front desk every morning so he wasn't distracted. Others are rather more unorthodox. Patrick Marber, for example, devoted several weeks here partly to playing poker – leading to his first play, *Dealer's Choice*, in which the game plays a key part.

A theatrical workout

If you look at the NT and the size of its theatres – 450, 892 and 1,150 seats respectively – no commercial producer is going to readily programme a new play into a 900-seater and yet that is what we are tasked with doing. So, if we want to see new voices, new forms, new anything, then we absolutely have to have a space where artists can come to gain a sort of theatrical muscle mass and try things out. The support that playwrights can have here in development terms enables us to be more diverse in our programming.

— Emily McLaughlin, Head of New Work

In addition to the writers' rooms there are three studios of varying size that can be used for workshops, readings, rehearsals and devised drama. Sometimes people use the studio spaces for a specific project, but sometimes they simply want to try out an idea that might later blossom into a piece. A large-scale piece in need of development might be worked on here, bringing together artists with different skills to improvise from a script in the spirit of discovery. The Studio is also home to the annual directing course and to the meetings of the music theatre group, which explores new ways of making musicals and encourages writers to think about the genre (the ground-breaking musical *London Road* sprang out of a meeting between playwright Alecky Blythe and composer Adam Cork). Other producing houses from around the country can also apply to use a space within the Studio to develop a piece of work.

No judgement

I had been writing *Nine Night* on and off for four years before it landed at the NT Studio, and I had two workshops at the Studio before the play was produced in the Dorfman. Both were a few days, working with a director and cast of actors, some from the company performing at the NT at the time, and others brought in specifically for the workshop. I remember the feeling the night before the first workshop. All excitement had turned to dread: nerves I had never experienced, not even as an actor. But those nerves soon dissipated once I entered the room. It was clear from the off; this was a safe space, away from the pressure of a rehearsal room, and without judgement or expectation. It was a place to explore, where I could ask questions of the actors and them of me. It was an opportunity to deepen my understanding of the story I wanted to tell. It was an invaluable part of the development process, hearing the actors' insights and watching them breathe life into the characters – voices that had been kicking around in my head for years. It was exhilarating. It provided me with the momentum and confidence to dig deeper and further still.

— Natasha Gordon, playwright and actor

The Studio also houses a reference library, offices and meeting rooms, where a couple of artists might gather to work through new passages or knotty problems in a piece. It's a friendly, unpretentious, low-key place – ideal for making mistakes and making progress well away from the limelight.

The writer in the room

Patrick Marber has written for all three of the National's stages. His first work, *Dealer's Choice*, premiered in the Cottesloe in 1995, as did *Closer* two years later, and his 2015 drama *The Red Lion* opened in the Dorfman. But he has also written new versions of classic works for the Lyttelton – *Hedda Gabler* and *Three Days in the Country* – and adapted Ionesco's *Exit the King* for the Olivier. He has come to relish the challenge.

'When I started out, I was scared of big spaces,' Marber recalls. 'Now I feel very excited by them. And I want the plays to be able to play a big room, because I think it's a big test of a play. Can it communicate all the way to the back of the upper circle, under the overhang of the stalls…? Your relationship with the audience is very direct in the Lyttelton – it's a good house for comedy. And the writing needs to be bigger: audiences want to experience change of thought quickly on the line, not stumblingly so. That's magnified even more in the Olivier. The Olivier is a place for scale and direct thought and action – it's not a place for tea-cups! All three spaces at the National are fantastically challenging for writers.'

Of course, every writer and every play is different. Some plays take years to write; some arrive almost fully formed. Some playwrights submit a voluminous first draft with a view to pruning it down in workshops or rehearsals, others produce a much more concise drama at the first attempt. And writers might come up with something totally unexpected: when Nicholas Hytner chatted to the upcoming playwright James Graham about his ideas for a new play for the National, he did not anticipate that the young dramatist would want to write about murky

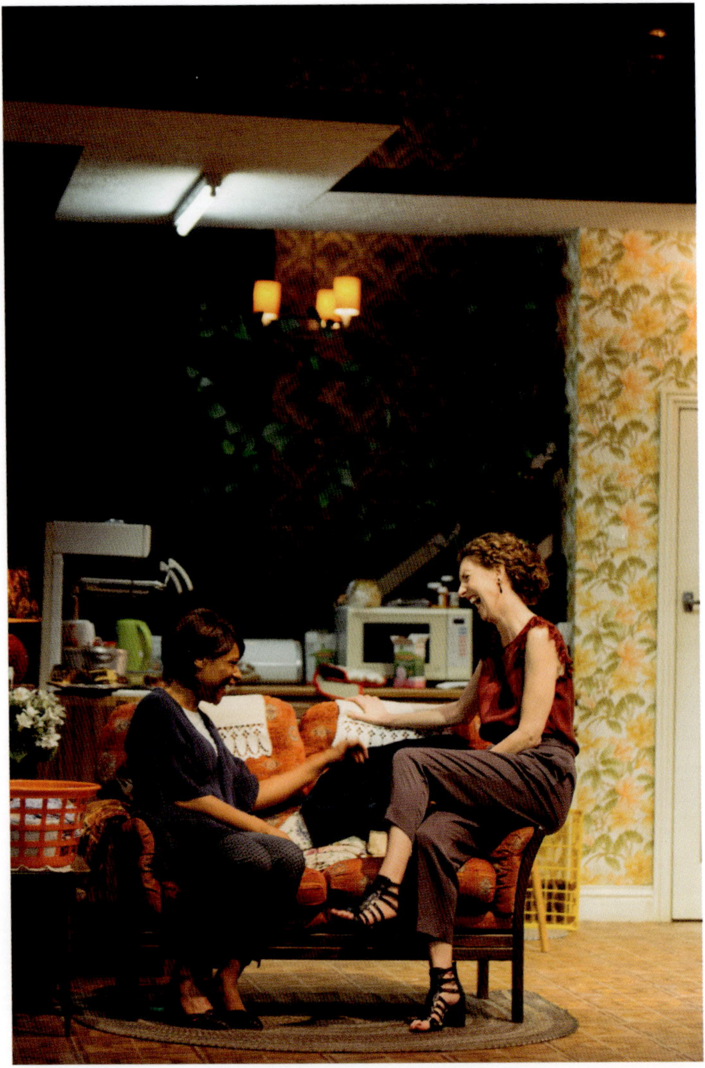

Franc Ashman and Hattie Ladbury in *Nine Night* (2018)

backroom politics in the 1970s. But that is what Graham suggested. Hytner went ahead and commissioned him – and the play, *This House*, turned out to be a huge hit.

Nearly all contemporary writers spend time in rehearsals, changing, adapting and developing their original script together with the actors and the director. Theatre is a collaborative art form at all levels. Just as a choreographer will work with the dancers in a room to create and perfect a sequence, so a dramatist will often work with the actors to bring characters to life and make dialogue believable. The idea of the solitary playwright producing a masterpiece in his or her garret, then handing it over to a creative team with instructions, is far from the reality, as Marber explains:

'A play is a living thing: you can't fix it until you hear it. You know when you're stubbing your toe on a sentence – if an actor can't say a line it probably means the line isn't very good. You need to be open to changes and you need to remind yourself you don't necessarily know best about your own play. There's nothing like the empowering feeling of changing a line in the room. Most writers, in my experience, enjoy being in the rehearsal room: they enjoy the feeling of the play changing live in front of them.'

That's not to say that a playwright will spend every day in rehearsal. Rehearsal periods tend to be between six and eight weeks (longer for a big musical), and generally the writer is needed near the beginning and the end of the process, to make changes, to work with the director on the vision and interpretation of the script and to respond to questions.

It's not just in rehearsal that a play can change, however. The other enormous factor in the equation is the audience, which is why the preview period on stage for a new piece of work is so crucial. It's only once the play is up and running in the theatre, with the actors in costume, the set in place and an audience responding to it, live, that its effectiveness can really be judged. Plays often change quite substantially between the first preview and the official opening night (during previews *War Horse* lost swathes of text in German and one poor actor lost nearly all his lines – but the play was the better for it).

So how long does it take to write a play? That depends enormously on the writer, the subject and the circumstances. Marber says that for him a play can spend years, or even decades, brewing, but that once he decides to write it he tries to get a first draft out quickly.

'I like to stalk a play, and creep up on it. And then at a certain point I've got enough notes and enough scenes in my head to go: "I've got you. I don't know what you are but I'm going to write you!"'

As Marber points out, a play is a living thing. The script, however brilliant it might be, is only the beginning of the story. While the writer hones his or her words, adds scenes and amends speeches, once a play has been programmed, teams of people throughout the building will work to bring it to life. Before the audience settles down to meet that finished work, there will need to be a set, costumes, lighting, sound, props and, first and foremost, a cast of actors and a director to lift it off the page.

Lucian Msamati in *Amadeus* (2016)

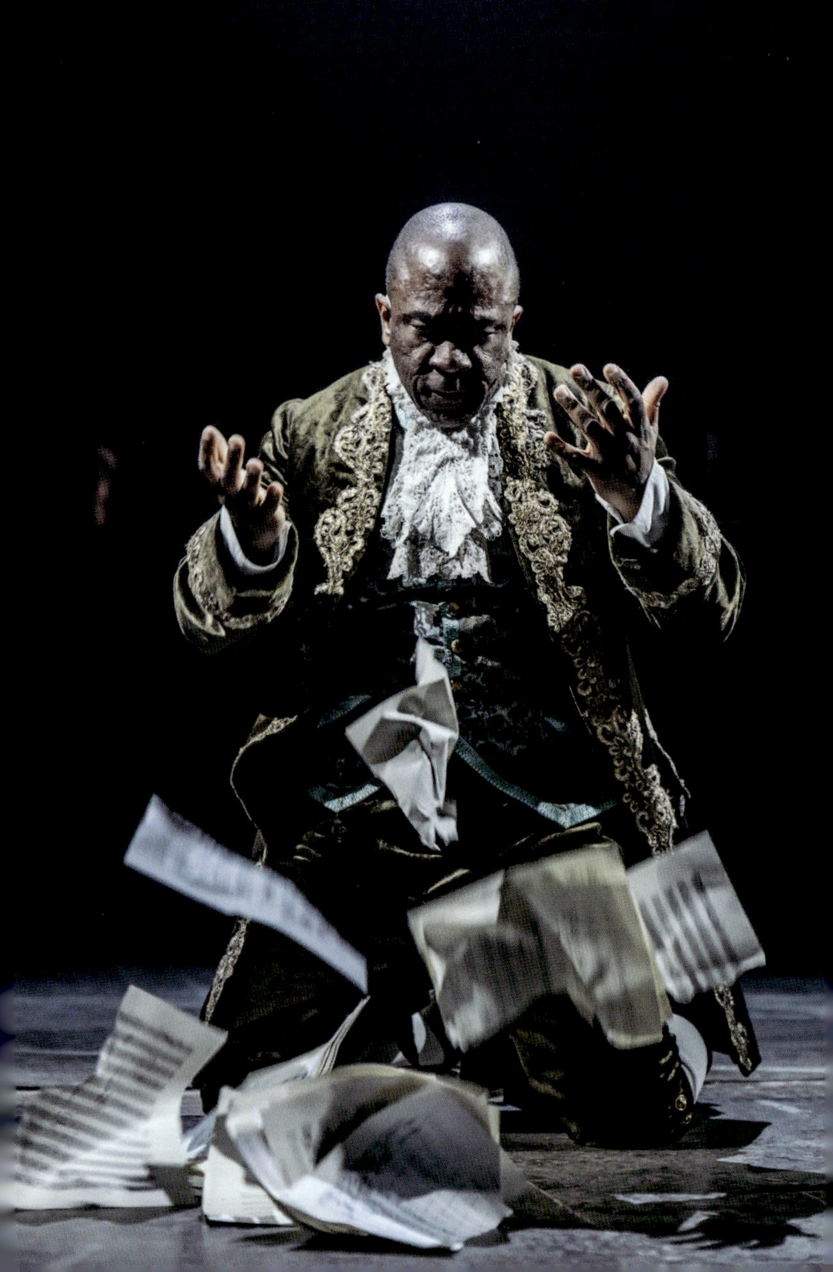

8. The Performances

In the rehearsal room

All productions start with a group of dedicated people in a room prepared to strive, sweat and even make fools of themselves in order to turn a script on a page into a living, breathing work of art. When it happens, it feels like magic. But great performances don't arrive fully formed – they are the result of weeks of work, of trying things out, of learning lines, of dark periods of doubt and exhilarating moments of discovery.

The process begins with the director. Sometimes a director approaches the theatre with an idea for a production; sometimes the theatre commissions a director to work on a specific text. If it's a play by a living writer, the two may well have worked together previously and have developed a mutual trust. And before anyone steps into a rehearsal room, the director has usually brought a designer on board and developed, with them, a vision of how the play might look and sound. Again, that common purpose and that relationship are so key to the success of the production that directors and designers often develop partnerships over the years, working together multiple times.

Also joining that team will be lighting and sound designers and possibly a choreographer, a composer and a movement director, all of whom will be working in tandem on the show as it makes its progress through the rehearsal period. Work on the set is often well under way before rehearsals begin. And then a couple of months before the show opens, the cast arrives. Whilst the technicians in the workshops hammer, weld and stitch together the physical world of the play, and whilst lighting and sound designers pore over computers, in the rehearsal rooms the actors begin to grapple with the task of becoming their characters.

Getting started

Before the first day of rehearsal, everyone has read the play several times: but how do we make sure we're all reading the *same* play? No play is really set where it pretends to be set: we're always in a world constructed by the writer's imagination, a world with its own rules, rituals and relationships. No two families are the same, let alone two societies. What might be permissible behaviour around one dinner table could be seen as hugely transgressive at another.

We know what each character *says* in the play because we're working from a script in which their dialogue has been recorded, but until we've spent some time asking establishing *how* this world functions it's hard to know which moments have weight. So I tend to approach the first phase of rehearsal from an anthropological perspective, assuming nothing about the inner workings of a social dynamic except that which we are able to observe.

What are the power hierarchies at play? What are the forms of capital which are most active in the drama and how is that capital exchanged? What are the borders and limits of the world and who is attempting to cross them? What are the rewards, sanctions and punishments in operation for the characters and how is justice dispensed? What, if anything, functions like a religion: where are the gods, and what are the totems which are most potent for this community?

These questions can apply just as readily to a play set around a family celebration as one which takes place before a great battle. If we're all in the same play, we can work together to tell the same story and to give the audience access to a complete world. And once we know the rules and the internal logic of the setting, the play often begins to direct itself.

— Lyndsey Turner, director

Putting flesh on the bones of script

For the cast, the journey begins with the first day of rehearsals, when the entire company comes together and everyone gets a chance to size up their working companions for the next few months. No matter how experienced you are, that moment is always nerve-racking, admits actor Lucian Msamati, who has appeared at the National several times and played the leading role of composer Antonio Salieri in the 2016 revival of *Amadeus*:

'The first day of rehearsals is always like going back to school,' Msamati says. 'It always is, no matter how long you have been in the business. As you get older, you end up feeling like the seniors coming back, so there is a certain comfort in that. But you still get butterflies knowing that you are setting off on a new journey. For me, personally, it's a very good sign, because it means I am going to have to work, to step out of my comfort zone. In rehearsal you have to become very intimate with strangers very quickly and to trust them very quickly.'

There's normally a 'meet and greet', not just with the rest of the cast but with everyone who will be working on the play in some way: the director, designer, choreographer, production manager, voice and movement coaches, stage managers, and members of many other departments in the building. Often the company will read through the play together for the first time (some directors ask actors to read roles other than those they will be playing, so that everyone has a more comprehensive understanding of the text). They will also look at the model box (a miniature mock-up of the set) to get a glimpse of the physical world they are going to inhabit on stage.

From then on, life gets busy. Rehearsals at the National tend to last between six and eight weeks, depending on the size and nature of the show (a big musical will need longer in the rehearsal room than an intimate play). At the end of every day actors get their 'call' for the next day – they are told when they need to be in the rehearsal room, depending on which scenes the director decides to work on. But absence from the rehearsal room doesn't mean a chance to chill out: those gaps soon fill up with costume and wig fittings, voice and movement work, publicity interviews and line learning. The timetable is tight and everyone is working to deadlines.

This is where the fact that everything is under one roof at the National Theatre makes a difference. Many theatre companies rehearse in spaces miles away from the workshops where the set, costumes and wigs are being created, miles too from the theatre in which they are going to perform. The NT, however, has six rehearsal rooms, which means everybody creating the show is in the same building as both the workshops and the theatres themselves. These are big airy spaces that can be adapted to fit the show.

Directors work in different ways: some like to analyse a text for a lengthy period before getting the cast up onto their feet, others prefer a physical approach from early on. Some like to play games to encourage the company to relax and lose their inhibitions (Ian Rickson, directing *The Red Lion* for the Dorfman in 2015, brought in a table-tennis table where the cast could loosen up by playing a few rounds). A few directors like actors to know all their lines at the outset; others, such as the renowned director Mike Leigh, work from improvisation. All rehearsal work is collaborative, but in some cases there isn't even a script until one is devised in the room.

The world of the play gradually shifts into and takes over the space: photographs and sketches on the wall act as inspiration or reminders of period; racks of clothes and piles of props appear – a vintage typewriter, a severed leg or, in the case of Katie Mitchell's 2009 staging of the Dr Seuss children's classic *The Cat in the Hat*, a fishbowl, a great deal of mess and a ridiculously baroque cleaning-up-machine. There may be musical instruments, items of food or even – as with *Peter Pan* in 2016 – ropes, pulleys, harnesses and flying gear courtesy of the Rigging department, in order to stage the famous flying sequences and aerial fights. If the play is a new work, you might find the writer hunched anxiously over rewrites (new plays often change a great deal during rehearsals as the playwright sees his or her work in action). But whatever the individual path of the production, there are always highs and lows.

'To begin with, you always feel like you've got loads of time,' says Lucian Msamati. 'Panic starts to set in in the middle of rehearsals – about three weeks in. It's the stage at which you are building a wall with bricks made of jelly. You know what it looks like and is supposed to feel like but it's not quite slotting into place. So the mid-point tends to be the first panic stage.

'There are also the dark days of doubt when you come "off book" [working with no script] for the first time,' he adds. 'That can feel quite exposing. You know what you want to say but you can't quite do it because you are trying to remember lines. And then the other panic stage, I would say, is the last week, just before you go into technical rehearsals and previews. Because you built this ship in the dockyard, as it were, and it's safe and comfortable and it works – in the rehearsal room with lines of tape and old bits of costume pulled out of the store. But suddenly you're going to suddenly be on the stage where you feel like a complete imposter.'

Getting technical

The move out of the rehearsal room and on to the stage for technical rehearsals brings a sharp change of gear. This is the first time the entire company works through the play *in situ* with the set, costumes, lighting and sound design. Technical rehearsals generally go on for several days – or even weeks – and involve painstaking work from early morning to late evening as the teams inch their way through thousands of sound and lighting cues and hundreds of costume changes.

This whole process became even more complex with Alan Ayckbourn's *House* and *Garden* (2000), two interlocking plays that told the same story

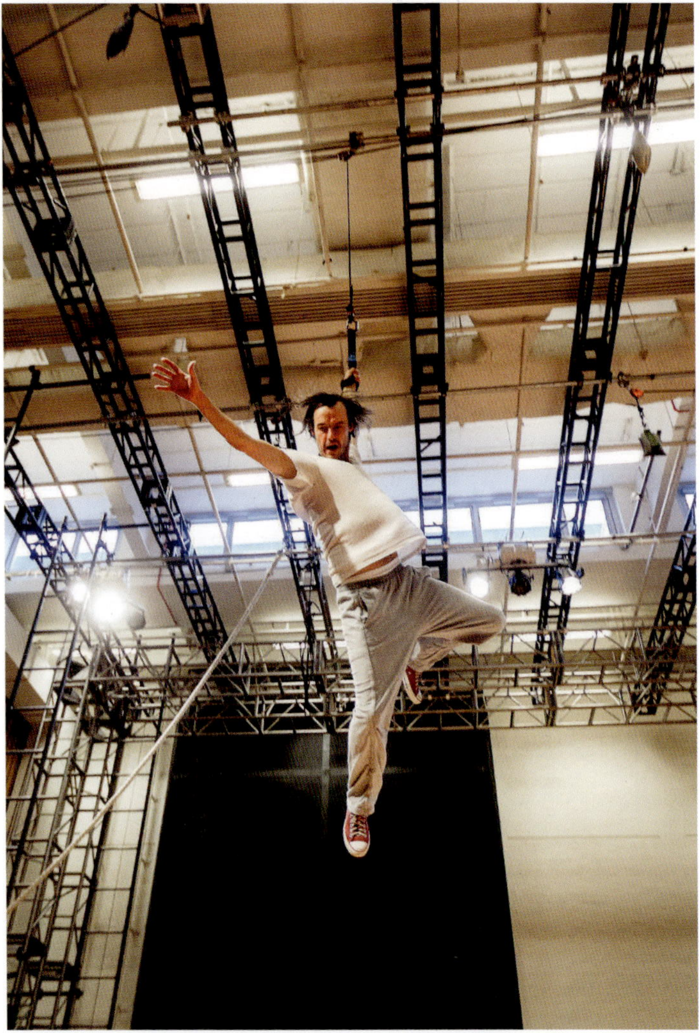

Paul Hilton rehearsing flying for *Peter Pan* (2016)

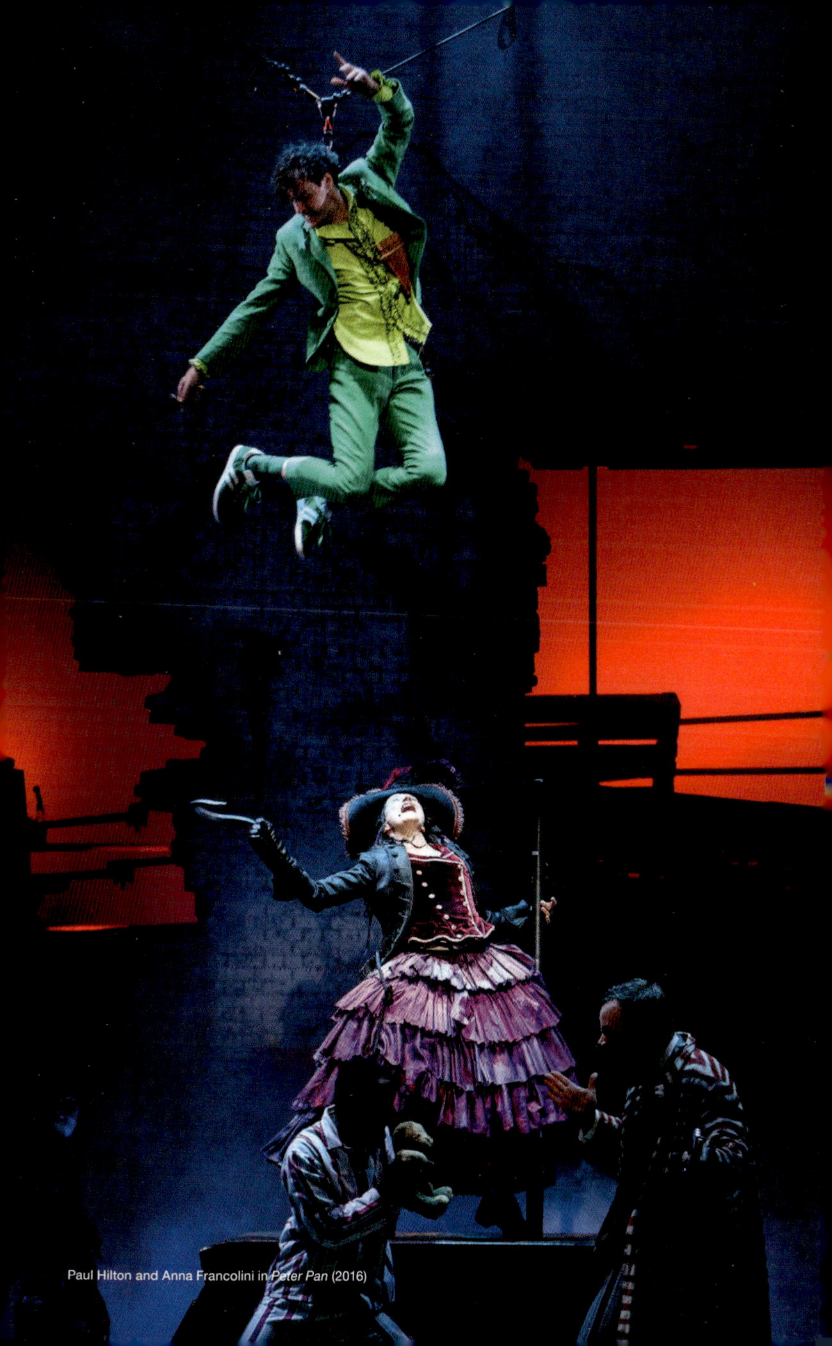

Paul Hilton and Anna Francolini in *Peter Pan* (2016)

from different angles and ran, simultaneously, in the Olivier and Lyttelton theatres. In his excellent and comprehensive book *The National Theatre Story* Daniel Rosenthal explains the precise timing required in both shows in order to make this work. The cast had to shift 36 times from one theatre to the other, mid-performance, which called for a mighty act of backstage organisation: the technicians marked out the route – 100 metres including several flights of stairs and multiple corridors – with yellow tape and there was a strict 'keep left' rule to avoid collisions between actors rushing from one stage to the other. It was precisely marshalled but even so, emergency bits of stage-business were developed that could be slotted into play if an actor was running late and there was even a special sound-effect – a barking off-stage dog – that could be deployed in case of emergency to warn those on stage to slow down. Fortunately, the 'emergency dog' was never needed.

'Techs' are generally both very tense and very tedious, particularly on a big show – those involved generally don't see sunlight for several days. In *Balancing Acts*, his memoir of his time at the National Theatre, Nicholas Hytner recalls the technical rehearsals for the mammoth staging of Philip Pullman's *His Dark Materials* being so stressful that he not only developed a sty on his eye but also damaged his wrist by storming out of the theatre in despair when a piece of scenery got stuck in the flies for the ninth time.

Everyone works very long shifts during techs so a good book and a sense of humour are useful companions. But it's also the point at which the full show really begins to emerge, as all the departments come together: actors see each other in their costumes for the first time and everyone encounters the set in all its glory.

Even after all that writing, building, crafting, rehearsing and reworking, there is still one key element missing to the show. The audience. Without an audience reaction, no play is complete. This is where previews come in. All productions at the National Theatre spend time 'in preview' (from a few days to a few weeks, depending on the show) before their official first night when the critics arrive. It's a chance to see what works and what doesn't and iron out teething problems. Productions often change a great deal during previews. In his diaries, Peter Hall describes how during an early preview of the original staging of *Amadeus* in 1979, the audience burst out laughing when a serious speech about a wind serenade came directly after Mozart had been blowing raspberries. 'It brought the house down. Amazingly not an actor, not a stage manager, nor Peter Shaffer, nor I have realised during rehearsal that that laugh was there,' he wrote. 'It must go.'

The mix of excitement and nerves flying around before the first ever performance of a show, combined with the fact that the dressing rooms all have windows that face onto a central well, has produced a unique National Theatre tradition. At the beginners' call (five minutes before curtain-up) all the actors in the theatre preparing for other shows bang on their dressing room windows to wish their fellow performers good luck (an act of solidarity repeated on press night and the last night). You can sometimes even hear this thunderous encouragement from nearby Waterloo Bridge.

While audiences for those early performances may get a more rough-cut version of the play, or even see something very different from later spectators, they have the satisfaction of knowing that they are the first to see it. They also play a crucial part in shaping the final product. For the actors, their presence is vital.

'There is nothing like the thrill of presenting something to an expectant audience for the first time,' says Lucian Msamati. 'The adrenalin rush, the joy, the excitement. That first time is very special. And of course it is the start of a whole new game because the audience is such a key part of it – you suddenly think "Oh I had no idea people would laugh there or be shocked there." The great joy and challenge for an actor is to get to a moment where you are completely open and it becomes second nature. It is those moments when beautiful things happen and fresh ideas come. Those are the moments you live for.'

A brilliant way to earn a living

Many directors do table work in rehearsal, sitting around a table and reading and talking through the play. That can be three days or it can be four weeks. I don't tend to do that; I don't find it particularly useful myself. But some very brilliant directors would completely disagree with me! In my rehearsals we usually talk through a bit of the script, try some things out, talk through it again, try it out again, leave it very loose and come back to it in a week's time.

I usually go through two books per project keeping track of what is happening and when. Those books contain drawings and notes and a table of scenes and sections. If I've done a rough run of the scene, it gets a dot beside it – there should be 6 dots for each scene before tech. So I have a snap shot at any time of what I still have to do: it forces you to be honest with yourself. We probably work through the whole play three times during the rehearsal process.

Throughout rehearsals I'll usually have two production meetings each week: one with the whole production team, run by the production manager, to make sure everything is going along ok and to flag up any issues; and another one with the creative team where we discuss what we are finding. It means that if you've lost track of the train coming down the track there are people around you who will say, 'Excuse me, we need these decisions to be made now!'

The technical rehearsal period is when your time management is at its most acute. If you've got eight tech sessions (a session being a morning, afternoon or evening), that's not very much to get through a big show. You've got to keep driving forward. So you get a lot done in previews. You work in the day and perform in the evening. A big show will often transform during the preview period.

As a director, the preview period is often when you discover just how good the writer is. And sometimes actors only really blossom in front of an audience. And costume designers only really get the opportunity to do their work once they can see it in the landscape of the theatre. So some things can change really radically during previews. And you have to be bold sometimes. If something doesn't work then you, as the director, have to make a decision about how to deal with it. Nobody else is going to be able to.

The great thing about being a director is that ultimately it's all your responsibility. You choose to work on this play, at this theatre, and do it in this way. Then you take it out in front of an audience. When it doesn't work, it's the most painful thing. But when it does, it's just the best feeling in the world – it's a brilliant way to earn a living.

— Rufus Norris, Director of the National Theatre

Inside a dressing room

While the audience are meeting friends, buying programmes and ordering interval drinks in the foyers, backstage the actors are getting ready to perform. All actors have their own personal routines; Lucian Msamati talks through his nightly preparations to play Salieri in *Amadeus* (2016).

'We have to be ready five minutes before curtain up. So for a 7.30 show we are in the wings, everybody ready to go, at 7.25. I usually try to get here at 6pm. I want to avoid traffic and stress. I try to make sure I've had a good meal before I come into the theatre: rice, chicken, vegetables or tuna and pasta.

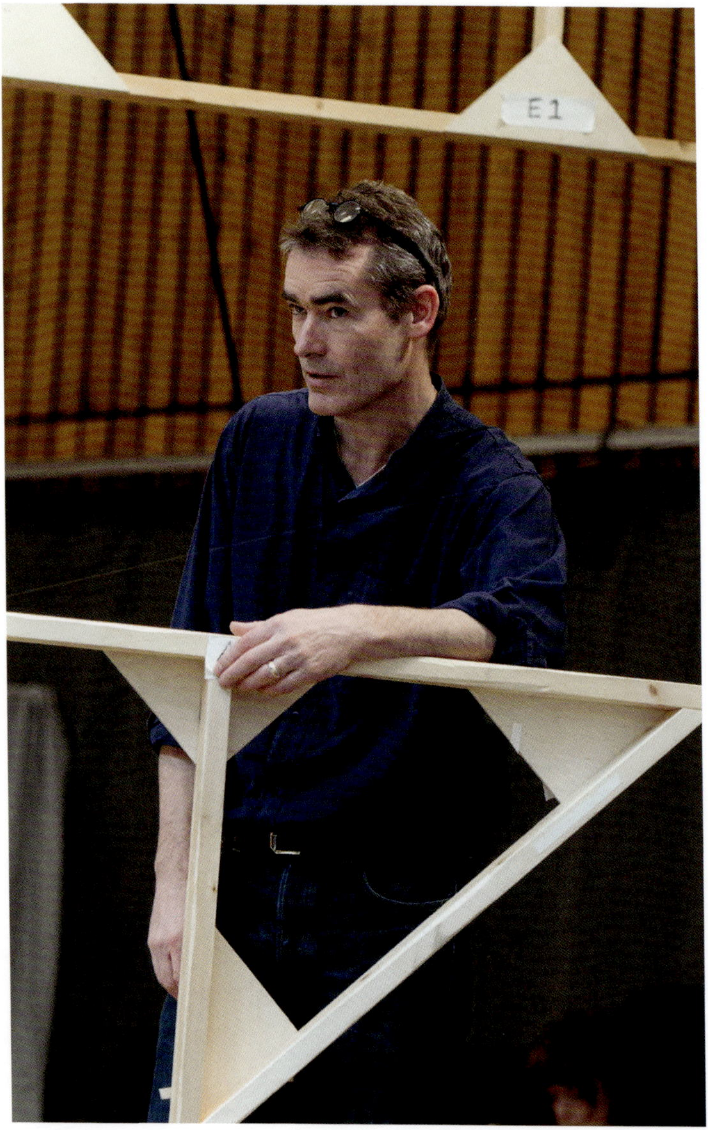

Rufus Norris, Director of the National Theatre, in rehearsal

'I will come in through the stage door and walk to the dressing room. I tend to get rid of the outside world: I put my coat, scarf and bag in the cupboard and lock them in out of sight. I will put the kettle on so I can get my various voice tonics prepared.

'Some people turn their dressing rooms into a home away from home, with photographs and so forth. I can completely understand that. You are going to spend a lot of time in here. It's your office really. I don't like clutter, so I don't like too many things. But there are certain important things that I do have: toothpaste, shaving foam, shower gel. I also keep my skipping ropes in a drawer for my warm-up. On the whiteboard I have written three words: "Have. Feel. Know." That is because there is a speech at the end of Act 1 in *Amadeus* with three very similar lines so this is an *aide memoire*.

'At about ten past six I will change into my warm-up gear then I head to the stage. The warm-up is a light exercise routine, vocal and physical: in order to get yourself ready for exertion you have to put yourself into a place where you break a light sweat. If you get over enthusiastic you can turn it into a workout. But it's not supposed to be a workout, it's just about getting the blood pumping – the show itself is going to be a workout. Everything you do beforehand is leading up to the show.

'After a warm-up of about 15 minutes, I leave the stage and have a shower – I must have a shower and get the room nice and steamy to warm up my voice. By now lots of people are going up and down the corridors, bringing snacks from the canteen, and you can hear the singers warming up. Then I begin the process of getting into costume, bit by bit. The dressers bring the costumes in to the room at about 6pm. I put the mic on myself. Carly (the dresser) will come in about 15 minutes before we go on to check the costume is all right – no tears etc. – and then she helps me to get into the shoes and puts on the ruff. It's all part of the ritual that I put those bits of the costume on at the very last minute because I don't like sitting around in someone else's clothes. At the five-minute call, so

7.20, members of WHAM [Wigs, Hair and Make-up] come in and do my make-up. I get "hero eyebrows" so that they stand out even at the back row. Then it's shoes, coat, bottle of water, let's go.

'I think there are two moments when I become Salieri. One is when the shoes are on: I look in the mirror and see the full costume. I think "Ok, there he is." And I really don't like to sit in the dressing room in costume. When it's time to go, it's time to go. The other moment is when the cue light comes on. The cue light is at the side of the stage next to the wheelchair [Salieri starts the play in a wheelchair]. Stuart, one of the assistant stage managers, gives me Salieri's coins. I count them out. Put them in the waistcoat pocket. That is our ritual. Then he gives me the cut-throat razor and hip flask of water. I get into the wheelchair, have a last drink of water, Stuart will ask me "Are you ready to go?"

'"Yes." And then he'll leave me.

'Then the cue light goes on and flashes red. You press the button to say "Right, I'm ready, I'm here in position", and then you just wait. And at that moment you are at the point of no return. You can hear the buzz of the audience. I'll offer up a little prayer of my own to the gods, the spirits, the ancestors, to myself, that I should be ready and open to do my job, to give my absolute best. And then I'll sit and wait and have my heart pounding in my ear. At that moment of silence and anticipation that's the point where I think to myself "Right, before you can go home tonight, you have got to go on this journey." And when the green light goes on, that's it: it's show time.'

Audrey Brisson in rehearsal for *Pinocchio* (2017)

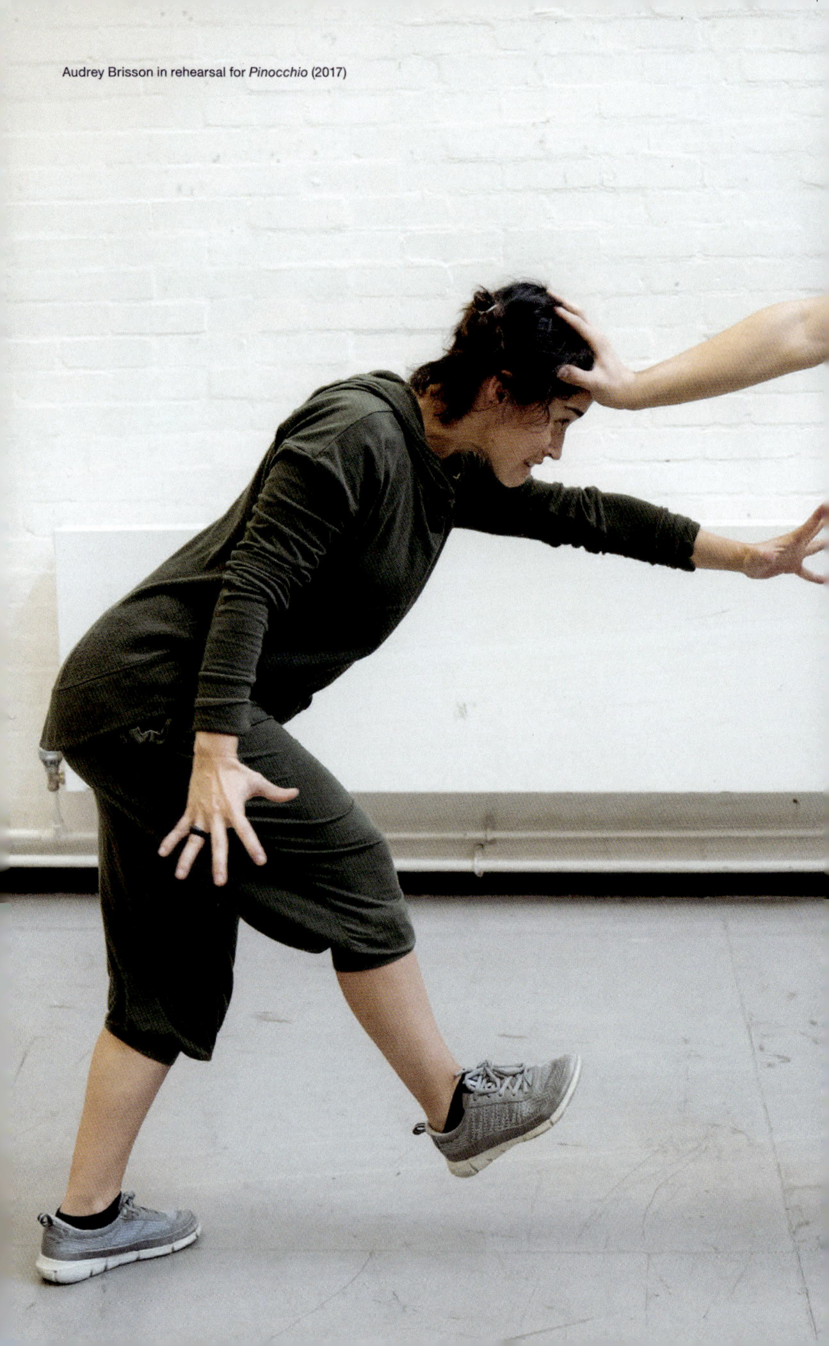

9.

Supporting Acts: Casting, Voice, Movement, Combat

Casting around – the role of the Casting department

Sitting in a theatre watching a show, you might spot someone along the row from you making notes. You'd probably assume they were a critic – and they might be. But there's another possibility. They might be a casting director.

Just as top football teams have scouts who travel the globe on the hunt for new players, so too the National Theatre has a unit dedicated to sniffing out new talent and finding potential stars for upcoming shows. When a play is programmed, nearly all directors will look to the Casting department to help with lists of actors they can call on to audition. The National Theatre employs over 350 actors a year and, while many directors have artists with whom they regularly collaborate and few would embark on a staging of, say, *Hamlet* or *King Lear* without a firm candidate for the lead role, most productions call for a mix of faces old and new. The Casting department have years of combined experience to draw on, together with a comprehensive cataloguing system and a good relationship with acting agencies. It's a job that calls for organisation, imagination and a sharp memory.

You also have to *really* like theatre. Casting directors spend at least three nights a week watching plays – from big West End shows to tiny fringe productions and drama school showcases. They observe both those in the lead roles and the supporting cast too, keeping an eye on newcomers but also on experienced actors to see how they are developing or changing. The idea is to be as sure as possible of an actor's range and potential before they are invited to audition.

If an actor is called for an audition, members of the Casting department often meet them, answer their questions and try to put them at their ease. It's in everyone's interests for them to feel confident and ready to demonstrate what they can do.

'You try set up a situation in audition where everyone gives of their best – director and actor,' says former Head of Casting, Wendy Spon. 'Diplomacy is quite a big part of your job. And you certainly feel for people when they don't get the role. You feel responsible – that's why you go and see so much, you have to have an informed knowledge about an actor's capabilities.'

The different demands of the National's three performance spaces impact on the casting choices. Because the Dorfman is relatively small and intimate, you might take a risk on a young, less experienced actor. But you probably wouldn't put them into a lead part in the Olivier because holding that huge arena might be too much of a challenge for them at an early stage of their career, and, if things went wrong, such a big, public failure could be damaging and demoralising to them.

In a sense, a casting director operates as a matchmaker, trying to use what they know about the director and the actor to create the perfect fit. What counts is not so much their own opinion of who would best deliver the part but their ability to find someone who might meet the director's approach. When it goes wrong, it can be painful. But when everything clicks, says Spon, it's immensely rewarding.

'When Denise Gough did *People, Places and Things* [Duncan Macmillan's 2015 play about addiction] she was on the threshold of despairing about the industry. But lots of us had known she was talented and then she came in for that audition for that play and she absolutely took it. No-one else came anywhere near.'

Indeed, Gough's searing performance, playing a recovering addict, won her huge acclaim and multiple awards. She later said herself that she had been on the verge of giving up on acting.

Some jobs are particularly challenging for a casting director: finding two sets of actors who can convince as identical twins, for example, for Shakespeare's *Comedy of Errors*, in which much of the humour and confusion depends on the fact that other people can't tell them apart (for Dominic Cooke's 2011 production Lenny Henry and Chris Jarman played one set of siblings and Lucian Msamati and Daniel Poyser the other). It's equally tricky locating a brother, Sebastian, for Viola in *Twelfth Night* – someone who looks sufficiently like his sister that it leads to profound complications when she disguises herself as a man. Ben Mansfield matched Rebecca Hall in Peter Hall's 2011 production.

Characters such as Romeo and Juliet are also tricky because the actors need to be experienced enough to be able to carry the play while looking young enough to pass for teenagers. And then there is the question of historical dramas – just how much does an actor need to look like Soviet dictator Joseph Stalin (Simon Russell Beale pulled it off in John Hodge's *Collaborators* in 2011), say, or British Prime Minister Harold Macmillan (played by Jeremy Irons in Howard Brenton's 2008 play *Never So Good*)? However difficult the search may appear, the combined experience and instincts of the NT's Casting department gives them the best possible chance of fitting the right actor to the role.

Finding your voice – the role of the Voice department

Where does Hamlet start when he gives his crucial advice to the actors just before they perform the play with which he hopes to trap his murderous uncle? With the voice.

'Speak the speech, I pray you, as I pronounced it to you, trippingly on the tongue,' he says, effectively warning the star actor against too much booming and blustering or muttering and mumbling. Hamlet is clearly aware of just how powerful an instrument the voice can be and how important it is for an actor to use it well.

Those particular actors, a troupe of travelling players, would be highly unlikely to have a voice coach, but artists at the National Theatre are more fortunate. The Voice department plays an integral part in all productions, supporting the cast in using and caring for this vital tool. Their work falls into three main sections: looking after and maintaining the voice, working on the use of language in a play, and coaching dialects and accents.

Vocal health is at the heart of the work of the department. Regular vocal warm-ups keep actors' voices supple and help to protect them from damage and strain. In daily life, we tend to forget that the voice is a part of our body and that vocal cords respond, like other essential muscles, to care, support and exercise.

'Voice is a physical activity,' says Head of Voice, Jeannette Nelson. 'So we always start with some stretching and loosening of the body in order for the breath to flow freely and to open up the jaw and mouth and throat. Once we have had a stretch we turn our attention to the breath. We talk about supporting the voice – that's using the deepest muscles in the body to support the air flow. We want to make the voice sound as if it comes from the whole body not just the head or the brain – as if it is coming from deep within you and is therefore authentic. We talk about the resonance and the buzz of the voice, we open the voice out through open vowel sounds and then we finish up with articulation (clear enunciation). Breathing is crucial in terms of supporting the vibrating sound but also making it part of your whole body.'

'Pitch is very important too,' she adds. 'We work a lot with actors to make sure they're not just sitting in the low part of their voice: if you sit at the bottom it's very hard to project and it limits the range of intonation and expressiveness. You want to use the full range of your voice. We always like actors to start working from the centre of their range and then go above and below.'

Actors do frequent voice warm-ups and work regularly on technique and voice health. They are also encouraged to keep hydrated, partly by drinking enough water, but also using steam: the water hydrates from the inside and the steam from the outside. Each production also has its own particular vocal requirements. The voice coach allocated to the production will spend time in the rehearsal room listening to the actors as they rehearse. They will then work with them on vocal technique as well as with the text: exploring the way characters use language in the play, asking questions such as whether they are good listeners, play rhetorical games, or use language to avoid saying things.

Of course, audience tastes and expectations have developed in recent times: film and television mean that people tend now to look for more naturalistic and colloquial delivery than in previous ages of theatre, so it is important that actors have the technique to deliver that without losing audibility or dropping energy. Theatres have changed too: the old Victorian and Edwardian playhouses were full of material – velvet seats, carpets, flock wallpaper – all of which helped to keep the sound in the space. Modern theatres tend to be less plush – the National Theatre certainly is – which means that audiences have to work a little harder to hear everything. And each of the National's spaces brings its own specific challenges, as Nelson explains.

'You have to work hard in them – all of them, even the Dorfman which seems small and like a studio but actually isn't. The Lyttelton is the widest proscenium arch theatre in London. And with both the Lyttelton and the Olivier the deceptive thing is the seating: on the stage it looks as if the audience is coming to you – it feels more intimate than it does for the audience. So, with both of those theatres I always make sure the actors go into the auditorium as well and listen to each other, so they understand that sound doesn't travel out as easily as they might think.

'The Olivier is an epic space, it's there to tell the stories of heroes and heroines, and it really likes language. You have audience members all around you, so you need to be alert with your back as well as your face. In the Olivier you need all your technique. You can't get away with anything because of that shape – it's very exposing. And you need to embrace that exposure. You need to make sure you look at and see everybody in the auditorium. If there's a fourth wall in the Olivier, it's at the back of the stalls not at the edge of the stage. So actors going into the Olivier, even if they are used to big Victorian theatres, need to really up their game in terms of how they embrace the space with volume and with the energy of language. Nearly always they end up loving it.'

The third strand of work for the voice coaches is the use of dialect and accent. This particular skill is made easier than it used to be by the presence of the internet, which means that a voice coach doesn't necessarily have to jump on a train to the appropriate region and stand on a street corner recording local people in order to catch the exact dialect. Once they have found the correct accent for a particular character, the voice coach will break it down phonetically, though that doesn't mean that they will teach it that way. Actors are much more likely to get under the skin of a dialect if it is taught to them in creative terms, says Nelson. And period accents need to be tailored to sound authentic enough without becoming incomprehensible to the modern ear – it is after all a piece of theatre, not a research project.

'We talk a lot about historical influences on accent: landscape, industry, the way people live, their proximity to other people. All of these can affect the energy of a voice. A character working on the docks might need to be louder and clearer, for example, than someone living in a stately home, who tends to communicate with people in a domestic space. Actors find that kind of work more useful.'

Poetry in motion – the role of a movement director

We all know how important body language is in our daily lives. We instinctively judge whether someone is timid or confident, friendly or hostile, at ease or on edge depending on the way they stand, sit or direct their gaze. On stage this subtle physical language becomes a matter of choice not of instinct. And keeping a close eye on it is just one of the jobs of a movement director. Often he or she is on board from the first day of rehearsals, working closely with both cast and director on the non-verbal communication in the play. They consider how characters move, how they react to one another and to events, and how they can transmit their emotional condition physically to the entire audience – without grandiose gestures.

Falling to the ground and tearing at your clothes or smiting your brow in woe, as used to be the fashion in melodrama, will rarely raise more than a giggle in the audience these days. At the other end of the scale, details such as biting your lip to suggest worry or wrinkling your nose to convey disgust are unlikely to transmit to the back of the stalls.

For movement director Polly Bennett, it's about asking questions such as 'Where does anger sit in your body and how can you release it in a public way?' She will work closely with actors to find ways to express emotion physically so that they can internalise the movements and make them feel natural. It's important, she adds, not to give actors notes that amount simply to physical instructions as they will then play the movement rather than the intent. So, for example, if a director remarked that a character was blinking too often and wanted the actor to tone that movement down, rather than ask the actor to blink less, Bennett might encourage him or her to imagine that the character's thoughts were longer and their breaths were longer – both of which would result in less blinking without making the actor panic.

Movement can also be integral to the credibility of what is taking place on stage and play a big part in setting the scene. For example, it is no use dressing actors in starchy Edwardian collars or tight Victorian corsets if they then lounge about on chairs in the socially relaxed style of the 21st century. Class, culture and etiquette play a big role in the way characters move, sit and talk in period drama. Actors might have to get used to wearing long skirts or cloaks or bonnets, or carrying walking canes and top hats.

There are also plays that need subtle gradations of physical behaviour to suggest shifts in place or time within the action. One such was *The Great Wave*. Staged on a revolving set, the play jumped back and forth between Japan and North Korea, and the company needed a clear way to differentiate between the two.

'We had to make a distinction between Japan and North Korea that was inoffensive and rooted in truth,' recalls Bennett. 'And also possible for a group of East Asian actors from many different places to play and for the audience to understand. There couldn't be the note "do it Japanese" or "be more Korean". We had to be really articulate with what was happening. Otherwise you become very generalised.

'In our story Japan was a freer space and so we worked on small gestures and the etiquette of that social space. By contrast in North Korea the intention was often to keep your body out of space and kind of compact yourself. Actress Kirsty Rider had to play that she had been kidnapped from Japan and taken to North Korea. When we saw her there we didn't know what had happened *en route*. Had she been beaten? Raped even? Drugged? How might that affect her behaviour? In Kirsty's performance, she played that she wasn't able to focus – she was constantly really trying to focus her eyes. It meant that she was able to bring a practical technique to help express a very difficult situation.'

Alongside such specific tasks comes a lot more general work on the physical quality of the production – the shape and energy of the ensemble, the movement patterns, the scene changes. Movement directors also work on relaxing the company and put them at ease during early rehearsals to support better creativity. Like Nelson, Bennett explains that the National's three theatres all bring their own specific demands:

'In the Dorfman people can be all around you, either side of you and above you in the balcony. In the Lyttelton there are two levels and it's very easy to forget the audience members underneath the overhang of the circle. A lot of the work is about making people aware of the space and knowing how far away things are and where noise gets trapped. It's about getting actors to think in this huge sphere up and diagonally above their heads, so that their performance flies up into the air and reaches everyone, rather than going forward and staying in the little box around them.'

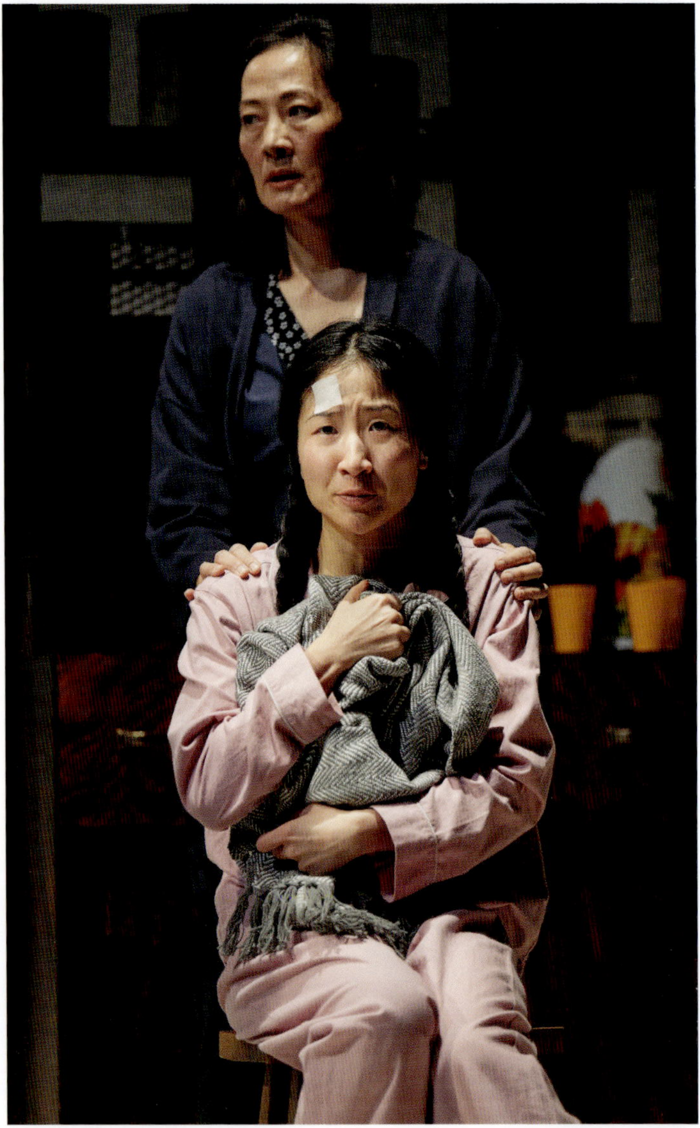

Rosalind Chao and Kae Alexander in *The Great Wave* (2018)

Fighting fit – the role of a fight director

One of the hardest physical things to do on stage is fight. Stage fights have to be convincing – there is nothing like an obviously fake slap to snap the audience out of the story – and the responsibility of making them look so rests with the fight director. She or he will work closely with the director and cast to shape and choreograph fights for the show.

In essence, stage combat is the opposite of the real thing. It has to look dangerous but be completely harmless. Where real fights tend to be spontaneous, violent and uncontrolled, stage fights have to be planned, safe and exact. And where people in a real scrap will be out to hurt one another, on stage they are actually working together to protect each other and themselves from getting hurt. So, every move, no matter how ad-hoc it looks, is planned and agreed with the actors, and routines are carefully rehearsed before the show so that everyone involved remembers exactly where they have to be.

'A stage fight is choreographed,' says fight director Kate Waters. 'It's like a dance and it has to be sustainable for eight shows a week. So, every move is completely and utterly worked out. I try to take it from a real situation – I'm always trying to make it not look staged – but what you see on stage is completely choreographed. If it's a messy fight, which lots of fights are, I've worked that out with the actors. What they can't do, once it is choreographed, is change it in the heat of the moment.'

There are techniques to make stage fights look as realistic as possible without anyone getting hurt. Actors can make a blow look hard by twisting their upper body and sending the punch from the torso rather than the arm. A punch will be masked (hidden by the body) to just miss the opponent's face. Meanwhile the recipient adds to the effect by recoiling on 'impact'. The 'knap' – the sound of a thump or slap – might be created by the actor delivering it slapping their own chest as they do it, or by the actor receiving it, or by someone else in the cast. Fight noises need to be perfectly timed and their source well-disguised in order to be believable. This is particularly tricky in an auditorium configured in the round so that there are audience members on all sides.

Stage fights can vary enormously, depending on the play and the scenario. Waters has choreographed a huge range of fights for the National Theatre: a formal fencing duel (for *Hamlet* in 2010), a large-scale brawl (*Othello*, 2013), a clumsy wrestling bout (*As You Like It*, 2015) and a messy, chaotic food fight (*Rules for Living*, 2015).

An important factor, she explains, is the reason for the fight and the story that is running through it. In *Othello*, a brawl breaks out because a bunch of soldiers are bored and frustrated and have been drinking but it also serves to reveal a frailty in the character Cassio. The fight Waters orchestrated attempted to reveal that – and contrasted markedly with the later struggle in the same play when Othello murders Desdemona in her bedchamber.

'You start by working out why the characters are motivated to fight,' says Waters. 'I carry a storyboard in my own head. I have a structure as to how I think it should feel. That's really important – the feel of it comes before the look.

'The first fight in *Othello* is a release for the men, stuck in that environment. It kicks off. There's a very important story, though, in that brawl, which I have to try and pinpoint all the way through it, which is Cassio's downfall. But those guys would all know how to fight and they don't mind getting stuck in. The killing of Desdemona, however, we kept very silent. She is fighting for her life. You do naturally fight for your life – your fight/flight instinct comes into play.'

By contrast, the punch-up in Sam Holcroft's comedy *Rules for Living* was an exceptionally chaotic and messy affair that erupted at a family Christmas lunch and culminated with one character pouring a jug of gravy over the head of another. It needed to be driven by deep feeling while also being ridiculous, funny and clumsily executed. Waters explains that the fight she designed was deliberately bad:

'Those characters wouldn't know how to fight. But it was a release for them – it was something they needed to do. So just getting them running around and throwing ineffectual kicks was perfect for those characters.'

In that fight the characters seized whatever was to hand to use as a weapon – mostly, because it was a Christmas lunch, pieces of food. But frequently fights involve more serious weaponry. Putting a weapon into an actor's hand creates another level of risk: fight directors work closely with both the Armoury and Special Effects department and the Wigs, Hair and Make-up department to ensure that the weapon is used safely and the effects are believable. Swords are particularly dangerous – even a blunted rapier could cause a great deal of harm if it hit someone in the eye or ear.

When Waters created the duel scene between Hamlet and Laertes at the end of Nicholas Hytner's staging of *Hamlet* (2010), she began with a formal fencing bout, with both characters obeying the rules. Then, as the contest shifted into a fight to the death between the two men, so did the fight: they ripped off their masks and became reckless. But both the elegant fencing section and the messier, more desperate fight were carefully choreographed and rehearsed.

As Fortinbras walked in at the end of that fight and of that production of *Hamlet*, his entrance marked the conclusion to one of Shakespeare's greatest tragedies. But it was also the final act in a process that had started with tentative discussions between the director Nicholas Hytner and the actor Rory Kinnear, then progressed, as do all plays staged at the National Theatre, through programming discussions, casting, rehearsals, voice sessions, movement consultation, fight lessons and the daily preparations to deliver the best performance possible.

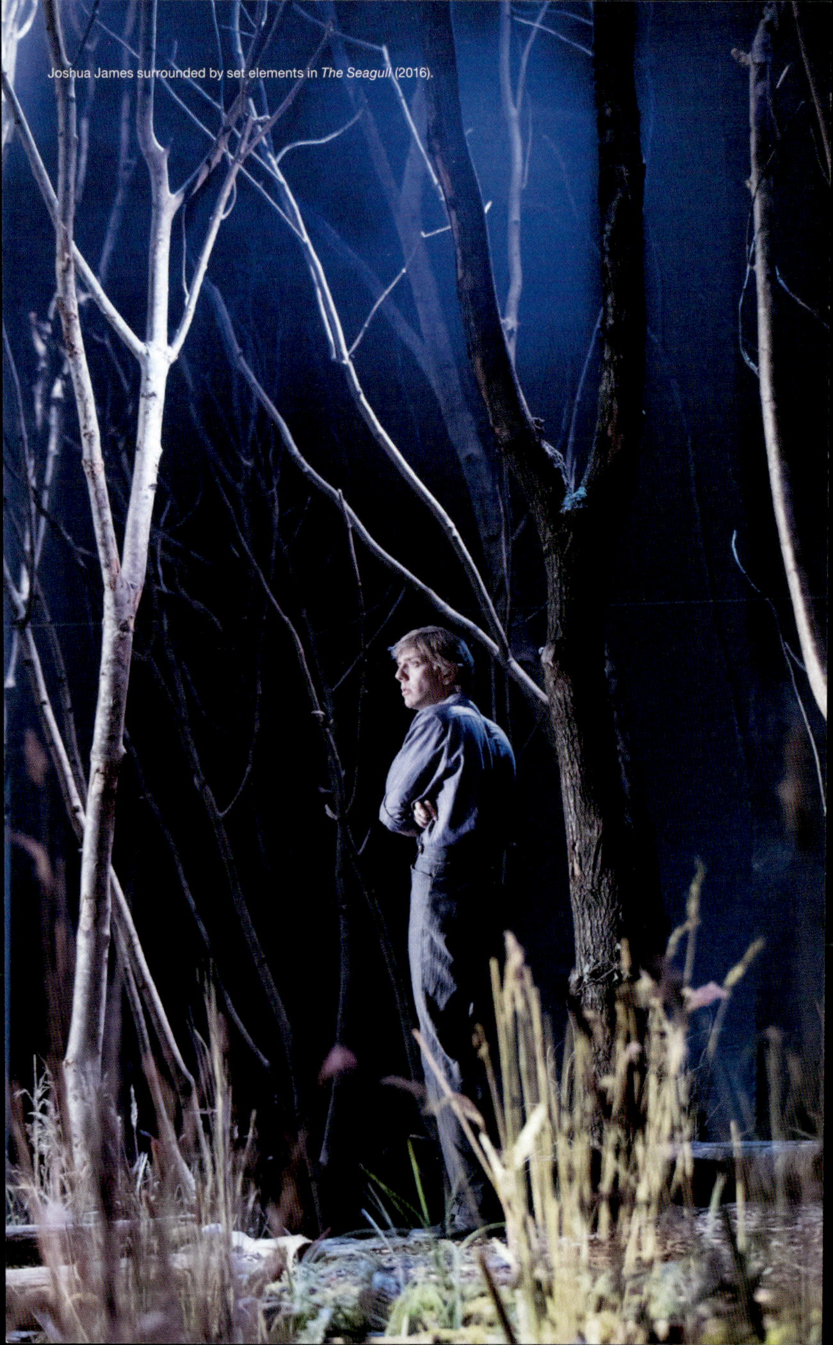

Joshua James surrounded by set elements in *The Seagull* (2016).

10.
The Set

Setting the scene

When audiences walked into the auditorium for the 2012 premiere of James Graham's *This House*, they found themselves not in the theatre, but in the House of Commons Chamber. Designer Rae Smith had transformed the space into the familiar interior of the Palace of Westminster. There was great delight as some audience members took their seats on replica versions of the famous green benches ranged on either side of the stage: spectators could imagine themselves as Members of Parliament following a debate and ready to interject with a barbed quip.

It was a hugely enjoyable set, perfect for Graham's political farce. But it did more than just set the scene. It emphasised the adversarial nature of British politics (key to Graham's play) and it wrapped the audience in the world of the drama. It was at once practical, immersive and symbolic and, as such, a prime example of just how crucial a role set design can play in a show.

Gone are the days when a respectable set involved a pair of French windows, a drinks cabinet and a bookcase that stayed more or less in place when a character slammed the door. The set is now a key element of any production: the designer is often the first associate the director signs up – the person responsible for bringing to life the world the dramatist has created.

The job of the designer

Everybody works differently, but I'll be trying to get to the centre of the piece and what that's about. There might be a particular moment that feels like the core of it, or a strong theme. I look at a whole lot of images – it's like a treasure hunt sometimes trying to find images that resonate with the story. I feel like I'm excavating, trying to get to the heart of it.

But that process doesn't happen in isolation. A lot of a designer's job is trying to listen to what the director wants. Some directors have a very clear idea of the way they want to do something. Others don't. Sometimes just putting things in a model box can spark off a bit of a journey. You try to be open and listen. You're trying to find your way through it together.

With *Dara* [a 2015 staging of Shahid Nadeem's play set in 17th-century India] I did a lot of research into the history. I found some pictures of windows cut out in Islamic patterns which let the light through. On stage they became screens that enabled the action to move around within quite a real space of steps and marble.

A lot of the time that's an issue you're trying to solve: how you move from one place to the next on stage. You're trying to find a physical visual language that allows for those transitions to be very fluid.

The initial period is often meetings, meetings, meetings and looking at visual references. Then when you've got the overall concept of what you're trying to do visually, you present it to [everyone in] the building, talk through the practicalities of it, the budgets, the cost implications of making it.

Then it is handed over to the different departments – the costumes and scenic workshops and prop shops. The technical drawings are drawn up and you'll have meetings with the Scenic departments over elements of the set. If you have done the costumes as well, you're up in the Costume department meeting the supervisors, choosing the fabrics etc. You have to make a lot of decisions and sometimes you don't know the answer until you see the samples.

So you are in and out of the building going through each of the elements that you designed and getting them translated to the larger scale. Then you get to the fit-up [when the set is assembled on the stage] and you come in during that in case there is anything that needs sorting before the technical rehearsal starts. And then you see it with the lighting and the sound and the actors. That's slightly terrifying, but it's also a lovely moment.

— Katrina Lindsay, Designer

Sets can range from the literal (the extraordinarily detailed and accurate cross-section of the ship in Lizzie Clachan's design for *Treasure Island*, 2014) to the abstract (2018's post-apocalyptic *Macbeth* design by Rae Smith was dominated by a huge steel ramp), from the complex (the multiple interiors concealed and revealed by sliding screens designed by Bunny Christie for *The Red Barn*, 2016) to the stark and simple (Bob Crowley's sweeping sea, sky and rock design for *Phèdre,* in 2009, featuring just six chairs).

Sets can be completely central to understanding the play – as in Christie's 'magic-box' set for *The Curious Incident of the Dog in the Night-Time* (2012) which, together with Finn Ross' video design, helped to take you into the protagonist Christopher's mind to share his experience of the world. Set design these days often involves a complex interplay between physical objects and sophisticated projection. It has to be imaginative, it has to be on budget – and it has to work.

Responsibility for the second two ingredients of that recipe lies with the Construction department, whose home is a set of vast, airy, interconnected workshops that run along the back of the theatre building. So huge is this space that it actually has an internal street alongside it, called Drum Road, which connects the theatres, rehearsal spaces and workshops and, as its name suggests, leads to the Olivier drum revolve.

In this department you'll find the welding, engineering, sawing, hammering and painting that go into creating a make-believe world on stage – the hard graft behind the magic. Amid the concentrated activity you might see curious mementoes from earlier shows: the handsome equine frame of a *War Horse* puppet hanging in the corridor; a huge stuffed pig that didn't make it in to *Common*; giant bits of puppet from *Pinocchio*. It's a place both very down-to-earth and a bit surreal.

There's a core team of 26 in the workshops, but this can expand up to over 40 at peak times. They build 75–80 per cent of the scenery, try to paint 100 per cent of it and see one set though the workshop every ten days. There are always multiple sets being built alongside one another so careful planning and timetabling is important.

The set's journey from page to stage begins in the drawing room, where project draughters break down the images and models provided by the designer into technical and bench drawings from which the construction team can work. The project draughters work with scenic heads of department and rigging and stage supervisors to work out all the basic engineering questions such as whether the set will be made from metal or timber, how sturdy it needs to be (will people walk on it?), how light it needs to be (will it get moved or flown in from above?), and how it will be put together and taken apart. The heaviest piece ever flown in the theatre was the front half of a house: it weighed four and a half tons – the equivalent of half an adult hippopotamus.

Heavy metal

Once drawings have been sent down to the benches, work can begin. Stage sets, like buildings, are constructed from the frame outwards, so the first port of call is often the metal workshop: a place that more closely resembles a factory workspace than a theatre, lined with stacks of steel bars and busy with welding, cutting and shaping. Many contemporary sets are now constructed on metal frames; 50 years ago they would have been made of timber. Steel is stronger, safer and more durable. Moreover, it has become much cheaper than it was several decades ago: in 2018 a six-metre bar of steel only cost around £10–£12. Another reason for the change is that design itself has evolved: sets are often bigger, more elaborate, more technical and are required to take more weight than once was the case. The metalwork team have to build things that people can walk on, climb on and live in and that can be quickly assembled and disassembled.

The metal the team use is relatively lightweight – of the type developed for gates and railings – and comes in straight bars. They then have to cut, weld, bend and punch holes in it to achieve the shapes required.

Into the wood

Generally speaking, the metalwork frames of sets are then clad in timber and painted. So the next stop for a set is often the carpentry workshop. It's here that the houses, rooms, doors and windows you see on stage begin to emerge, as carpenters choose from a variety of types of wood in a range of thicknesses to create everything from building walls to tiny structures.

The detailed work is done by skilled carpenters but as time is crucial and always tight, the workshop also has several advanced pieces of gadgetry that can speed through some of the most labour-intensive and time-consuming tasks. One is a vertical panel saw that can rapidly slice wood.

The other is a remarkable CNC (Computer Numerical Control) router: a computer-driven cutting machine bigger than a double bed that, in a few minutes, can produce hundreds of precisely cut, complex shapes that would otherwise have required hours and hours employing a hand-held jigsaw. Extremely useful for any job that requires many exact replicas (stair risers, for example), the router can also generate 3D carvings, creating complex forms – such as animals – and even relief work as seen on the walls in the 2018 *Antony and Cleopatra*.

The diary of a set

We work back from the fit-up date, which, on a big Olivier show, is usually three weeks before press night.

Ideally, 20 weeks before that we see the white card model, that's when the designer and director show us the broad concept of what they are trying to deliver on stage, and we have read the play so we can understand how they are trying to tell the story. We then go away and do a rough costing and an estimate of how long the set will take to build. That gives us a period of about two weeks to flag up complicated pieces of scenery (if they require automation, for example) and put large pieces out to contract. We have to consider how the whole thing is going to be assembled: we don't want people to be climbing up the back or hanging off of objects if we can possibly help it – safety management is very important. So, one early question is: 'How does that get put together?' Everything you build has to come apart and come out of the theatre really easily too, because of the repertory system (we try to strip down and replace a set within four to five hours).

The creative team go away with our feedback and come back about six weeks later (so about 12 weeks before the fit-up) with the final model, having taken the points on board. Each production has a tracking document and each project is broken down into elements: there will be a leading scenic art supervisor, construction supervisor and project draughtsperson. Then we start scheduling when the work is going to go through: we can say we need the floor finalised by this point, the stage left wall by this point etc.

Rehearsals can be anything from 11 weeks to just four, so we focus on stuff needed in the rehearsal room first. We try to do floors really early. The bigger, more complex bits of scenery that require proper assembly come later in the process. By that point we're also talking to the Sound, Video, Lighting and Automation departments. Complex bits of scenery require input from a great number of people.

— Darren Joyce, former Head of Construction

For the carpentry workshop, the most challenging sets to make tend to be those that involve curves and circles. Es Devlin's ground-breaking design for Lindsey Ferrentino's *Ugly Lies the Bone* (2017), for example, presented some massive technical hurdles. The show explored the emerging use of virtual reality to assist pain management (it focused on a soldier who had suffered severe burns in the line of duty) and immersed the audience in a virtual world by means of a vast, wraparound set. This took the form of an enormous curved bowl that filled the whole width and height of the Lyttelton stage. It was studded with 2,000 tiny 3D houses and could be transformed by the use of video projections into a beautiful winter landscape.

It was made by affixing curved pieces of plywood, cut by the router, onto a heavy steel structure. Because of the steep curve, the carpenters and scenic artists were faced with a wall that was travelling both upwards and away from them. Unable to walk far up it, they had to learn to abseil in order to work on the higher parts of the structure. They also had to fix the miniature houses in place with absolute precision, otherwise they would not marry up with the video and the whole illusion would be ruined. It was a job that called for ingenuity, accuracy, collaboration and extreme patience.

Reality can pose just as many headaches as virtual reality sometimes. For the exquisite *Young Chekhov* trilogy in 2016, the design, construction and scenic art teams had to turn the Olivier stage into a 19th-century Russian estate, complete with lake, which contained 35,000 litres of water, chlorinated to avoid attracting unwelcome microbes (particularly important since actors had to wade through it at various points). Whenever a set includes a pool or a lake, the workshop technicians need to build sealed, watertight troughs to contain it.

A brush with frame

After weeks of construction work, you might have the basic shape of the scalloped walls of a 17th-century Mughal palace for *Dara* (2015), or the dwellings of a small Jewish *shtetl* for *Travelling Light* (2012), or the interior of a 1950s Salford flat for *A Taste of Honey* (2014), but they remain just shells until they have visited the Scenic Studio (also called the Paint Frame).

This huge, open, brightly lit hangar at the far end of the workshops specialises, as its name suggests, in painting scenery. It's a space full of trestle tables, trolleys of paint pots and examples of different surface types (a piece of wall here, a tree trunk there). The 'frame' itself is vast: 30 x 11 metres, it runs the entire length of one wall and is several storeys tall. It is accessed by three platforms that track both vertically and horizontally, to carry the scenic artists anywhere on the whole expanse of a backdrop. The team use super-saturated pigments and emulsion paint, which can be mixed with water, flame retardant liquid and textures to adapt to the needs of a given job.

One of the main challenges in the paint frame is working out how to reproduce effects on a much larger scale than they were originally rendered. A mark on a design or in a model box might look very different when blown up to 25 times its original scale, but the final set needs to reproduce that same feel. Another challenge is that standing on the platform, very close to the work, artists cannot necessarily tell how it is going to look from metres away. For that reason, they often use a grid to plot what image goes where on the model and then reproduce that grid, on a much larger scale, on the actual piece of scenery.

A great deal of the work involves creating believable surfaces and textures on structures – creating the effect of wood, brick, marble, gold or tree bark. For this work they often use vac-form: heat-moulded plastic sheets similar to those used in biscuit tins and chocolate boxes that hold their shape but are very light.

This was crucial in the 2017 staging of *Follies*, which needed large, battered brick walls to create the feeling of an old theatre. The show was in the Olivier and mounted on top of the drum revolve, which can only support a certain weight, so the scenic artists in the paint frame had to make the walls look really solid and credible while keeping them as light as possible.

The questions scenic artists have for designers will often be practical, to establish what treatment a surface might receive during performance – will someone touch it, for example, or spill something on it? And they need to be sure that when pieces of scenery are being dismantled and reconstructed over the cycle of performances, the surfaces are not going to chip or flake. They also need to be aware of the way the textures and colours they use will look in the theatre environment itself, rather than in daylight.

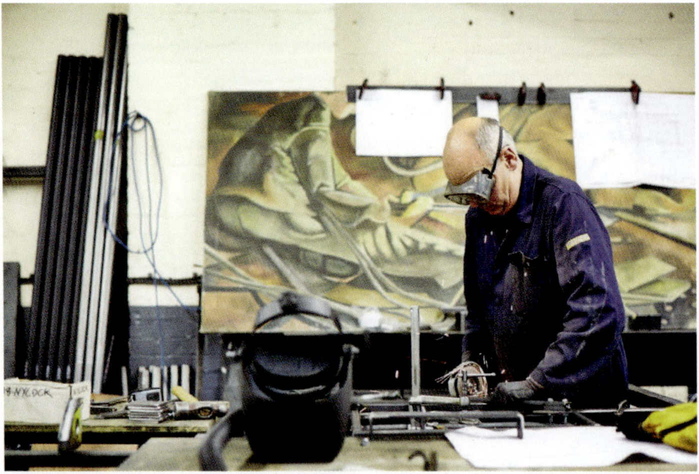

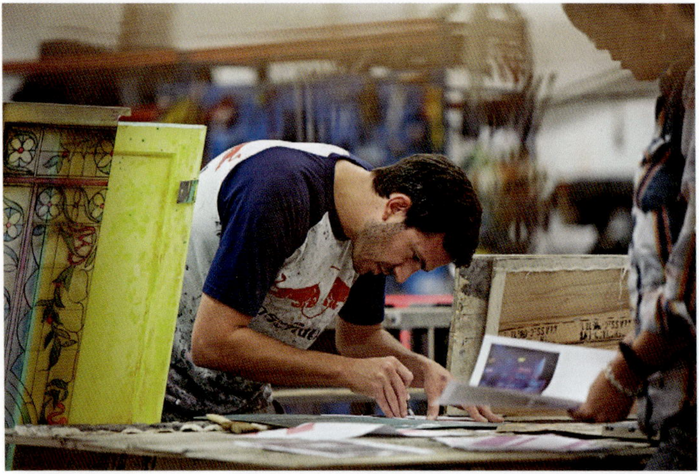

Set elements being worked on by members of the set construction and scenic art teams

Flash, bang, wallop

Deep within the National Theatre is a room lined with guns, spears and knives, where a man spends his days thinking about fights, setting things on fire and blowing things up. In any other context this would be deeply worrying. But at the NT it is essential because his job, as Senior Armourer, is to create special effects. Controlled chaos is often his mission.

Paul Wanklin is the go-to man for weaponry at the National and, like a fight director, one of his tasks is to ensure that all on-stage conflicts look dangerous but are in fact totally safe. The rows of guns on the wall – from modern machine guns to elderly blunderbusses, muskets and the kind of ornate pistols favoured by dashing, fictitious highwaymen – all achieve their effects by firing blanks. It still requires training for actors to learn how to hold them, however. For instance, you should never point even a fake gun at someone's face because even a blank can cause injury. Swords, meanwhile, are blunted and those knives that villainous characters drive into their victims' chests are either retractable, with a hollow handle, or have a hollow blade full of blood that oozes out when you squeeze the handle.

But however harmless, they need to work. If a gun doesn't go bang in a film you can just retake the scene; if it doesn't go bang on stage, it's very obvious and something of a disaster if the character on the receiving end is meant to have been shot dead.

And there is far more to the Armoury than a load of old ordnance. It's here that nearly all the special effects on stage are cooked up: pouring rain, blazing fires, pyrotechnics, boiling kettles, dancing tables, the sparks and jets of steam generated by the huge train in *Frankenstein* (2011) – they all come under the Armoury remit. 'I am basically a jack of all trades,' says Wanklin. 'If it's not anybody else's job: it's mine.'

Fire, surprisingly, is easier to handle than water. For a small flame you can use real fire: 'If we manage the risk you can just light a piece of paper and drop it into a metal bucket – so long as somebody is watching it. It's when you leave it and go out of the room that there is risk,' Wanklin explains.

But for a bigger conflagration, propane gas comes into play. At the end of Yaël Farber's major revival of Lorraine Hansberry's *Les Blancs* (2016), the house on stage caught fire. The set was made to accommodate having propane gas pumped into it, which looks very realistic when it burns (it has a yellow flame) but is easy to control and can be instantly switched on and off, both essential qualities if you want to avoid incinerating the set and burning down the theatre.

Water, as we've already mentioned, is more wayward and is likely to trickle to where it is not wanted. Sometimes the crew actually plumb things in – flushing toilets, running showers and so forth – though quite often a tap on a kitchen sink will simply be powered by a hidden garden sprayer. More problematic are bodies of water, such as lakes and pools, and pouring rain. Getting the rain onto the stage is quite easy – it is sprayed down – but collecting it can be tricky, as can preventing it from dripping when it is not wanted. And if it is not sufficiently backlit, even the wettest downpour won't be clearly visible from the stalls.

Wanklin is also in charge of props that move or do tricks. The table in *Pinocchio* (2017) from which objects would randomly fall or jump was his work, as was the desk in *wonder.land* (2015) that the head teacher could drive around the stage. In fact *wonder.land* called for a lot of crazy props. Wanklin also devised a moving bed, operated by radio control. But as he explains, radio-controlled props don't always behave as you want them to.

'The radio-controlled bed didn't work all the time because there's so much radio now in theatre. If it picked up a wrong signal it wouldn't do what you wanted it to do. It worked nine times out of ten but then every so often it did something strange. One night it just kept going round and round and round – the crew had to go on and grab it.'

That was nothing compared to the giant animatronic crocodile in one staging of *Peter Pan* (1997), however, which sometimes – alarmingly – seemed to develop a mind of its own:

'In *Peter Pan* we had a massive radio-controlled crocodile,' says Wanklin. 'That thing used to pick up the taxis going past and twitch and do all sorts of things. Its mouth would be opening and closing and you had no control over it. A lot of the time the old tricks are the best. The more complicated you make things, the more likely they are to go wrong, so I always try to keep things simple. If I can fire a pyro with a wire and a cable, I'll do it like that. If I have to use radio I will use radio, but if I can just hide a wire somewhere, that's how I'll do it.'

Pulling it all together

As Head of Production, I have overall responsibility for the production managers, for the Drawing department, the Construction workshops, the Props shop, the Costume shops, the Running Wardrobe and the Armoury... so half of the making end of the business (the Lighting and Sound and Video departments are under the Technical Director).

One of the key things I do is to shepherd the productions through from their very early beginnings to their delivery on stage. Essentially, it's about matching artistic ambition with available resource. It's maintaining the vision that is behind the work and balancing that with the budget. We are all here to try and deliver what the writer, director and designer want.

The process is very intense. We're building this whole physical world on stage and every detail of that is important. So we get it drawn, we get it costed, we go back and forth, making it hit the budget, then we start building it. The lighting designer and sound designer get involved; rehearsals start; the whole technical team meets at least once a week *en masse* with the director to discuss what's happened in rehearsals; the props get slowly fed into rehearsal and actors come in and out of rehearsals for costume and wig fittings. Everything is very precisely scheduled – it has to be to squeeze all the work in – and then after six weeks we get to the point where we fit up the show. It's a fairly tense technical period from the moment of putting the set into the theatre to the first preview: a lot of people working long days for a couple of weeks. And then we get to preview and that's the real test, seeing it in front of an audience.

My other job is to support the production managers and to have an overview of how it's all working. Production managers come under a lot of pressure, because they have the artists who want their vision delivered, the producer who wants it produced on budget and the technicians who want to go home on time. It's like building a house in two or three days. It can get very emotional because people get tired and stressed and there's a lot of fear. You are exposing yourself and your work to the public and it's quite terrifying. And it's such a subjective thing. If there was an algorithm for the perfect show and someone had discovered it they would be very rich. But there's no way of guaranteeing that. There's a strange alchemy to it – and that's the joy of it.

— Paul Handley, Head of Production

Adrian Scarborough in *Exit the King* with prop telescope (2018)

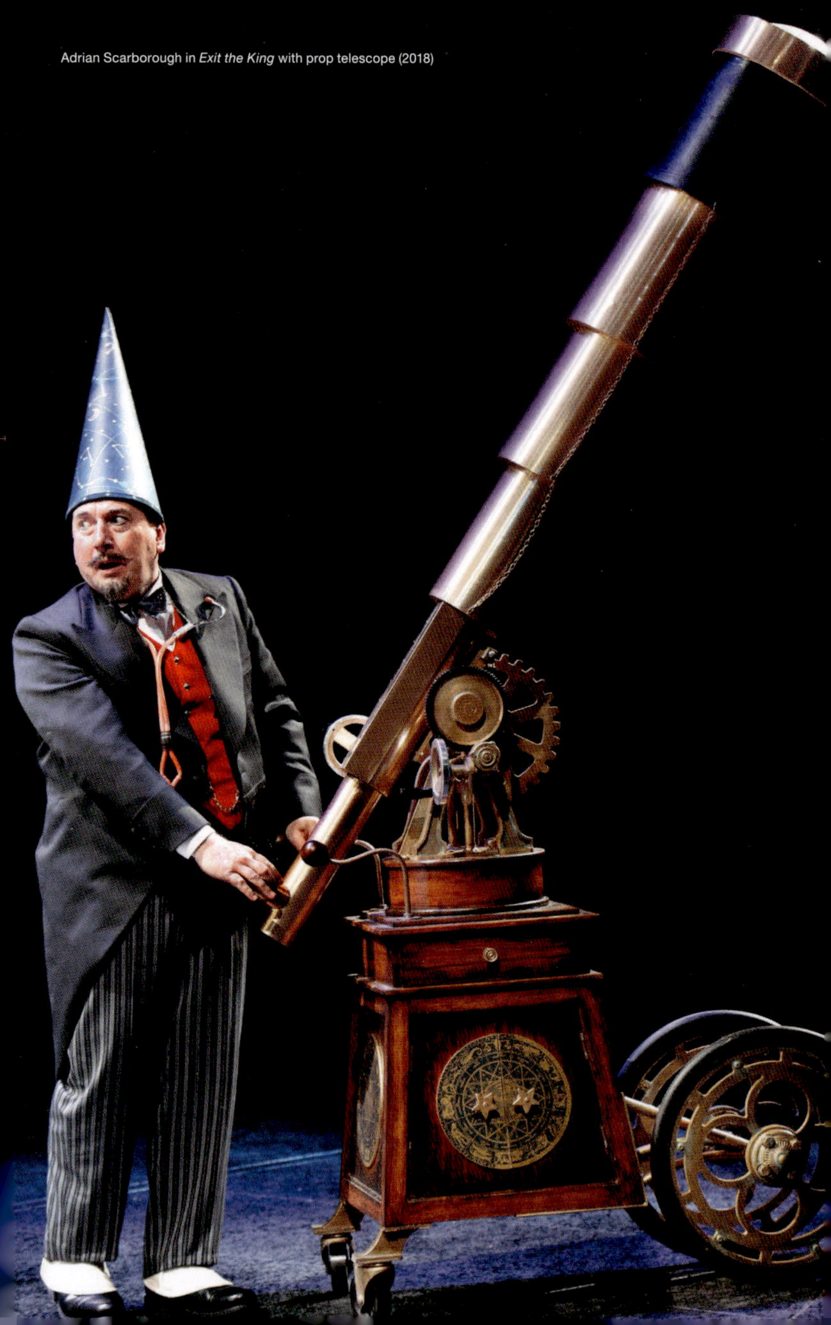

11.
The Props

Hot properties

Long John Silver without the parrot, Hamlet without the skull, Hedda Gabler without the pistols – many characters would be nothing without their signature props. And whether it's a talking crow, a treasure map, a severed head or a collapsing table, the job of making them comes down to the Props department.

Stage properties, to give them their unabbreviated name, can be as incidental as a pen or a cup, or as central to the whole production as the giant puppets in the 2017 staging of *Pinocchio* (in a twist on the original, all the characters were played by puppets, except for Pinocchio himself). They can be anything from the tiniest key to a huge First World War cannon (as was created for a 2014 production of Sean O'Casey's *The Silver Tassie*) – but whatever their nature they have to both convince the audience and function properly. That cannon looked immensely heavy and realistic but was, in fact, made of materials such as cardboard and foam, so that the cast could drag it onto the stage easily.

Much as with the set builders, the first question the props makers ask of designers is usually: what is going to happen to the items on stage? If there is a table, does somebody stand on it? Does a drunken character get up and dance on it? If there is a chair, does it have to wobble or get thrown around? Does that vase get broken? Does that toaster burst into flames? Props may have to be reinforced, made to fall apart and be reassembled, or be made in multiple copies if they need to get smashed to smithereens. Among the Props department are trained carpenters, cabinet makers and sculptors, though unlike many people trained in those crafts they often have to create objects that deliberately malfunction.

Artistry, craft and thoughtful care

Over the 17 productions I've directed at the National Theatre the thing that has struck me most is the quiet brilliance of the folks labouring in the Scenic Studio, the Props and Costume departments. No show is possible without their artistry, craft and thoughtful care. For me their industry is the bedrock upon which all the work at the National Theatre is built and I've often wanted to steal whole departments away with me to work on shows in other houses. I certainly would not have been able to build an aesthetic or experiment with different ways of theatre-making without their daring, patience and imagination.

— Katie Mitchell, director

Many props play a key role in the narrative of a play, so it is imperative that they perform correctly. No actor wants to go for a huge, dramatic exit only to find the door knob come off in their hand, or discover, mid-seduction scene, that the lighter with which they were about to light their sweetheart's cigarette doesn't work. Getting things unfastened is often particularly challenging – actors might have to unlock a chest, or quickly release a prisoner from his manacles and all the dramatic tension will be lost if they are fumbling around with keys for ages. In fact, locked items tends to be fixed shut with Velcro, which is easy to rip apart.

Cooking up food is a major part of the Props department's work. Many lavish banquets are in fact constructed from foam and plaster. If the food gets eaten on stage, however, then it needs to be real – but it also needs to be something the actor can cope with every night for months and months. In Sarah Kane's play *Cleansed*, for example, one character is forced to eat a whole box of chocolates. This might sound like the ideal part, until you realise that the actor has to chain-consume sweets and still speak – making chewy caramels a no-no – and also still fit into his costume at the end of the run. For Katie Mitchell's 2016 of production of *Cleansed*, the Props department dipped grapes in chocolate – they still looked the part but were lower calorie and easy to swallow. Meanwhile, in *Rules for Living* (2015), the cast used a real cooked turkey for the central Christmas dinner because it needed to be carved every performance, which would have been very challenging with a model.

There are tricks of the trade for alcohol, too. When we see an actor downing a bottle of whisky and then staggering off stage, the impression of profound inebriation is down to good acting and a solution of burnt sugar and water: a much better bet for getting through both the script and the drive home intact. And those celebratory glasses of champagne seen at many an on-stage wedding? Ginger ale. It's a matter of balancing the needs of the plot with the actor's comfort and, often, dietary requirements.

The Props department, like the Costumes department, will select a props supervisor to work on every show, who will work out the budget for the props with the designer, and assess what needs making and what needs buying. Many contemporary items can be bought and, if necessary, modified. Before the existence of the internet, every prop department would have 'bibles' of information about where to find arcane objects such as ancient samovars, period perambulators, old packs of playing cards and disused typewriters. Even now, the internet can only take you so far: prop makers are still experts on where the best flea-markets are held and on all the curious little out-of-the-way shops where you can find specialist items.

Feathering the nest

You find props in places you never would have imagined. For feathers, for example, your best bet is to go down a little road in the East End of London and up some rickety old stairs where you'll find these men with boxes and boxes of them. They are wholesale feather sellers: they have feathers you'd never even dreamed of ...

– Nicky Holderness, Head of Props

Brushing with death

You sometimes need a strong stomach to work in the Props department. One area the Props department know more about than many of us would wish to is taxidermy, as sometimes they have to use real dead animals (ethically sourced) either on stage or as casts for models.

Most animal corpses are made on site, however. In the 2014 production of Shakespeare's *King Lear*, the king's boisterous knights made one entrance with a slain stag slung from a pole. The stag looked so realistic that some audience members wrote in to complain about the use of a real animal. Happily, the Props department had not gone off deer hunting to acquire this magnificent beast – the misapprehension arose because it was so meticulously constructed. The team had made the body themselves, building it from the skeleton outwards: first bones, then muscles, then fur. They used different types of foam, from very hard foam that holds its shape and can be carved, almost like balsa wood, to make the bones, to softer upholstery foam for muscles and fat, and then covered the whole thing with fake fur.

Dead characters present another problem. If an unfortunate individual loses their head, literally, the item has to look realistic but the actor involved naturally can't donate their own. But to make it look realistic, however, and not like a generic severed head, it's often best to make a live cast of the actor.

The props team will first encase the actor's hair in a swimmer's cap to protect it, coat the face, neck and upper chest in Vaseline, and then apply the thick, runny alginate all over the face and head (avoiding blocking the nostrils). An alginate is similar to the substance used by dentists to make dental imprints – after just five minutes it will start to firm up. The team next applies soaked plaster bandages all over the alginate coating. Once the substance has hardened completely, the mould can gently be prised free of the actor's head, and filled with quick-setting modelling plaster, which, when hard, will present a perfect copy of the actor's head.

Similar techniques are used for other body parts, though since these are more interchangeable, the department does keep many body part moulds (along with food moulds) in the small room where they do all their plaster-casting. Stacked high with the moulds for feet, arms, grapes, chocolates and joints of ham, it looks like a rather strange and higgledy-piggledy version of a sculpture gallery.

Props can play a major part in a show or just a tiny role. But either way, it is essential to keep track of them once the show is up and running. At that point, responsibility for them shifts to the stage managers, who have to ensure that all props are present and correct and in the right place, at the start of every performance. They run a 'props table' in the wings off-stage where a space for every item is marked out with masking tape. One of their biggest challenges is to make sure they retrieve small props from distracted actors as they make their exits, so they don't end up rummaging around in the dressing rooms for a letter, dagger or handkerchief that might be the lynchpin of the plot.

Follies actor Kate Parr helped by a member of Wardrobe

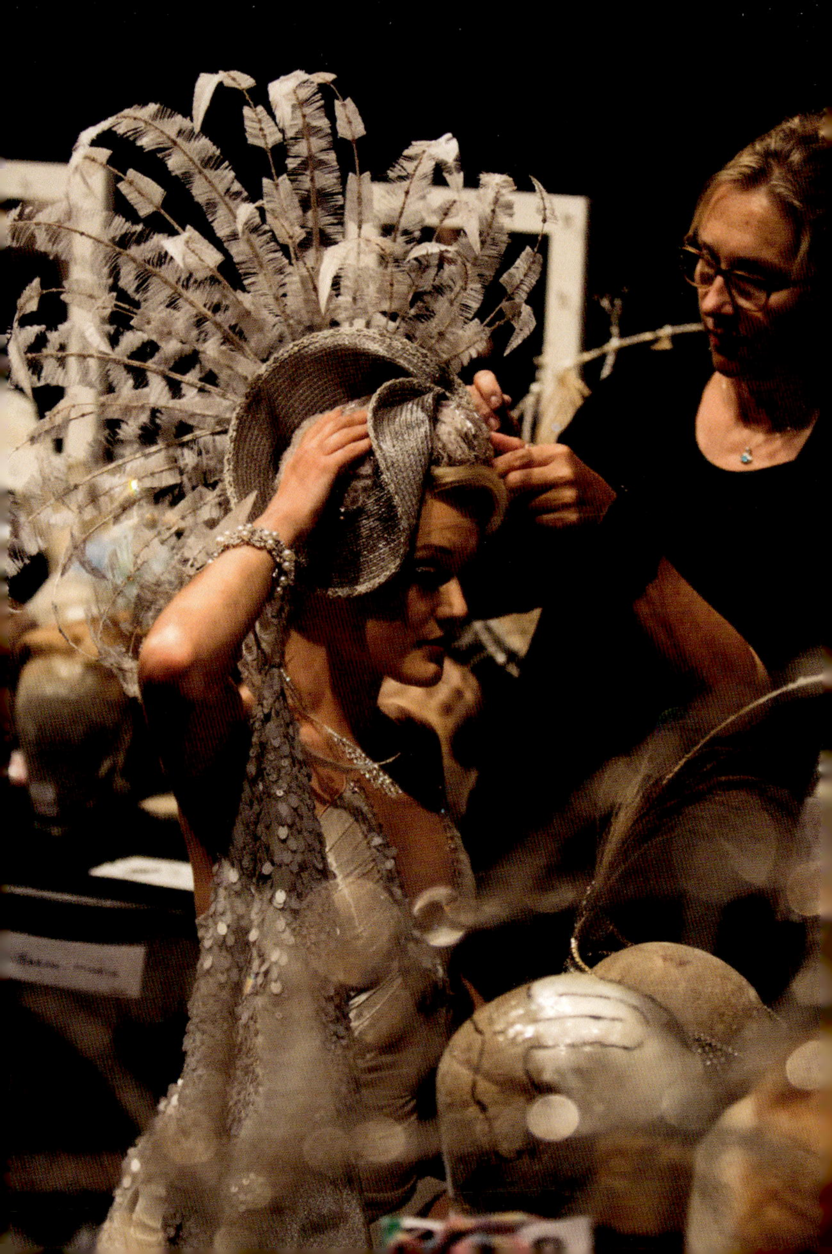

12. The Costumes

No detail too small

A bespoke tailor on Savile Row needs to be able to make a suit that fits its intended wearer perfectly. A costume cutter at the National Theatre needs to be able to do exactly the same. The big difference, however, is that the stage suit might have to *look* priceless but be produced on a tight budget. Meanwhile the wearer might also have to fight a duel every night, climb through a window, dance frenetically, or get covered in mud.

Costume-making requires a blend of ingenuity, versatility, authenticity and practicality. The NT's Costume department creates clothes for approximately 24 shows each year, ranging from huge, fantastical and historical epics to modern three-handers. They generally have the costumes for at least two or three shows being prepared at any one time, with others being maintained for performances every night.

No design is too outlandish: for the theatre's 2015 staging of the musical *wonder.land* the Costume department created a giant, bulbous caterpillar and massive, metallic, concertina-like pantaloons for Tweedledum and Tweedledee. No detail is too small. For Laura Wade's 1950s-nostalgic *Home, I'm Darling* in 2018, even the buttons on Judy's pink cardigan and the strap on her tiny gold watch were perfect vintage items.

The Costume department is in charge of every aspect of the costumes from the moment the designer walks through the door to the moment the actors walk onto the stage. They work in close contact with the Running Wardrobe department, who take charge of the costumes once a show goes on stage, storing and maintaining them throughout the run, supporting the actors and assisting them in 'quick changes' during the show. They launder and repair items, ensuring that they look as good for the final performance as they did for the first.

Patterns and plans

Before so much as a pin is wielded or a stitch sewn, crucial meetings take place. First, the costume designer for the show (for many productions a single designer works on both set and costumes, but sometimes the costume designer and set designer are separate people) will meet the Head of Costume and the costume supervisor contracted to that production. Like supervisors in other making departments, their role is to work alongside the designer and to turn their designs into reality. He or she will decide who is going to make the costumes (in collaboration with the in-house workroom), find outside makers if there are too many to complete in-house, consider what can be bought, and where, and work out how to manage the budget. Everything has to be precisely costed, down to the price of socks, handkerchiefs and hat-pins.

All the costume supervisors are based in one small room in the Costume department. Here they hold meetings with freelance makers, experiment with ideas and store fabric samples and shopping. The variety of shows in rehearsal at any one time makes this a wonderfully eclectic space: one desk might be overflowing with feather boas, sequins and sheer stockings, while another is covered with samples of armour and military camouflage. Nearby is the pattern room: a small studio lined with thick box files, folders and catalogues of everything from fabric samples, to handbags, to armour suppliers. Supervisors and designers can retreat in here to peruse the options available. Three whole box files are devoted solely to lace, four to stockings and long hose, several more to millinery and jewellery. Another room is an Aladdin's cave of sundries stored in boxes – handbags, hosiery, hats, brooches, buttons, lace, strings of pearls – which designers can pull out and rummage through to find the look that works best.

The costume supervisors also liaise with the stage managers to schedule costume fittings for actors throughout rehearsals. Performers try on the costumes at various stages in the process of construction so that the makers can fit them accurately and ensure that they are comfortable and fit for purpose. Scheduling can be challenging, as actors are busy in rehearsals and may also have fight calls, make-up and wig fittings, vocal sessions and publicity duties to juggle. Fittings take place in two rooms, each dominated by huge floor-to-ceiling mirrors, racks of clothes and shoeboxes. The rooms are fitted with stage lighting, so that costumes can be examined in conditions similar to those on stage. Here actors, together with a handful of people including the designer, costume supervisor, costume maker and wig supervisor, will see the look of their character emerge for the first time. It can be quite a delicate moment, as the actor is often stripping off and trying both their costume and their character on for size, so the numbers in attendance are kept to a minimum.

The costume team also receive notes from rehearsals every day, in case changes to the staging have an impact on what is being made – the inclusion of a fight, for instance, might necessitate alteration of the costume. New plays offer a particular challenge – often the script itself changes during the rehearsal process: characters might change sex or grow older, new characters may be introduced or others cut out of the play completely. On average, the Costume department has between four and six weeks to find and make clothes, but on new work that period can shrink considerably.

Once a show migrates out of the rehearsal room and on to the stage to prepare for performance, the costume supervisor and designer will watch it together, studying the effect that lighting and distance might have on the look and colour of the costumes. Although the fitting rooms have stage lighting, final refinements may still have to be made. And there could be teething problems with clothes – particularly shoes – which only emerge once an actor is wearing them for several hours.

During the latter part of rehearsals, understudies also need to be considered – they might be smaller, taller or thinner than the actor they are covering, so need their own costumes. If there are musicians on stage, or if members of the technical crew come on to move things during the performance, they too may need something particular to wear. Meanwhile, actors' bodies can change: people might put on weight, lose weight or become pregnant during the run of the show, and their costumes need adapting. The Costume department can work on a costume several times throughout its life.

Pin and needles: tricks of the trade

Some costumes will be bought – especially those for contemporary plays. The department's buyers spend hours scouring high street stores, vintage stores, charity shops and websites and have an encyclopaedic knowledge not just of these, but of all the arcane places where you can buy fine fabrics, leather, buckles, handbag clasps and bishops' mitres.

Others, both modern and period, can be sourced from the National's Hire department warehouse. This huge storehouse in south London houses over 130,000 costumes, shoes, accessories and props. Each item is barcoded and catalogued with details of its size, colour, period, the show it originally came from, and the actor for whom it was made. It's an extraordinary resource, offering options and inspiration for designers, who trawl the rails looking for ideas. And it is used not just by the National, but by the wider industry: a costume that made its debut on the stage of Olivier might find a further life in a television series or in another theatre.

But while reusing old costumes can go a long way, a huge proportion still have to be made to order, in-house, in the long, brightly lit cutting room on the fourth floor. It is home to a permanent team of eight: including ladies' cutters, men's cutters (cutters being the heads of the teams), makers and those who work on alterations, amending bought clothes or items retrieved from the Hire department. At busy times, or when there is a particularly large show in preparation (the theatre's seminal 2017 production of Stephen Sondheim's musical *Follies*, for example, which required 133 costumes), the team will expand: up to six further spaces can be created on the end of extendable tables.

It's a cheerfully industrious space where light chatter is interspersed with the hiss of steam irons and the hum of sewing machines. The work varies enormously: you might find someone tailoring a regular pinstriped suit alongside someone stitching yards of delicate voile while someone else fashions a crinoline skirt with plastic boning.

The imagination and specialist knowledge needed for some costumes means that the cutters and makers are very much part of the creative process: a designer will come up with ideas, but the practicalities to do with how a costume is constructed and how it is worn – these can all be down to the invention of the makers. The more extraordinary the costume, the more imagination the maker will have to use to bring it into being.

Costumes can play a key role in establishing someone's character and in supporting a play's plot. Audiences will absorb a great deal of subliminal information about a character from the outfits they wear and the way they wear them. Do they look expensive or cheap, new or old, clean or dirty? As Polonius advises his son Laertes in *Hamlet*, 'the apparel oft proclaims the man'.

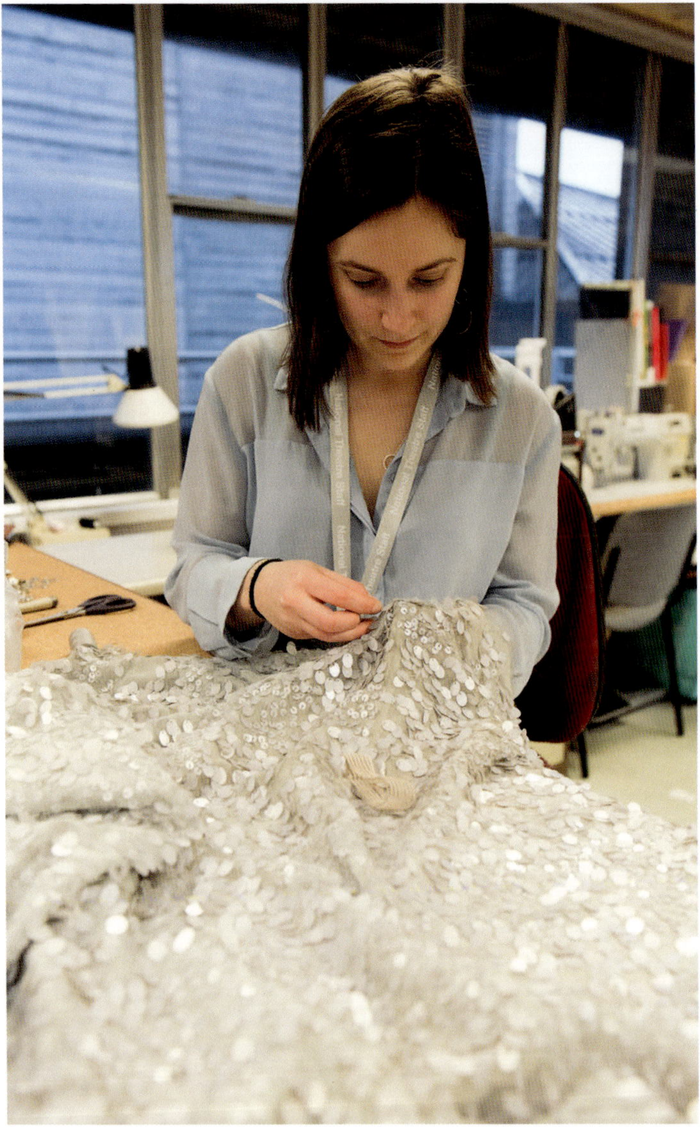

A member of the costume department at work

Storytelling through costume

When getting to understand the play one thing we always ask the designer is about the passage of time. Is the play set all on one day? Or do we meet characters again years later? If so, what is their situation? Are they on the up? Have they moved into a different social setting? How can we subtly express that in their clothes? A costume is part of the storytelling.

— Carol Lingwood, Head of Costume

People in real life don't tend to wear up-to-the-minute fashion every day: they may wear clothes they have gathered over a few years, or beloved favourites from a decade ago, and such clothes tend to look lived in. The Costume department is scrupulous about such details, working with designers on ensuring that characters look like genuine people from their era, rather than fashion models, and that their outfits have the right amount of wear and tear. The textile studio works on breaking them down, making them look worn and washed, rather than box-fresh.

For period costumes, the level of authentic detail can be incredible, right down to the underwear. An actor might have to take their outer garments off and change on stage, so the underwear has to be accurate for the period. Frequently for ladies the underwear affects the shape of the dress worn over the top: a 19th-century dress won't hang properly if it is not supported correctly underneath (although authenticity is not taken to the level of discomfort and corsets aren't made from whalebone as they were in the Victorian era – actors need to be able to breathe!).

Clothes also affect the way people move – as soon as an actor dons a corset, it makes her stand and walk differently. For this reason, actors often request an element of their costume to work with in the rehearsal room – a cape or a corset or a long skirt, for example, might help them to find their role. Some people also ask for shoes in rehearsals – perhaps to help them establish their character, perhaps to get used to the practicalities of wearing them.

Authenticity has to be matched with practicality: an actor might need to wear a smart shirt and tie, but he might also have to execute an energetic dance number, so the shirt needs to be built into his undergarments to prevent it from flapping out in the sort of undignified manner familiar at office parties. An actress might have to start a play in a sophisticated cocktail dress, but have to change off-stage into surgical scrubs in less than a minute for the next scene.

Costume makers build in all sorts of little tricks to help actors make such quick changes. They might thread elastic through a set of cuffs, so that an actor can push their hand through quickly, or in the place of shoelaces, so they can wriggle a foot in or out of a shoe more easily. Frequently, on a row of buttons, every other button doesn't do up, halving the time needed to remove the garment. There might even be tiny magnets lodged behind the buttons: the actor puts the item on; the magnets find each other and it's instantly done up. Costume makers rarely use Velcro, which is too noisy, or zips, which are too prone to breaking and too difficult to fix: if a zip breaks on a costume the actor is still wearing, they are trapped in it, perhaps ruining the next scene.

Dyeing for a change

A key role in the creation of costumes falls to the textile studio, an extraordinary little room – part kitchen, part laboratory. The walls are lined with tins of coloured powder, which the two full-time dyeing experts, cook up in the correct quantities for the strength of dye they need. On the large stoves sit small pans, in which the dyes are mixed, and huge vats full of swirling pigment, which bubble like witches' cauldrons. The fabrics are bundled into these and soaked in dye. Above rises a vast extractor chimney to draw away the fumes.

It's a wonderful combination of old techniques and new. Although the room resembles a medieval alchemist's lair, with its steaming pots and brightly coloured potions, it's important for the department to stay on top of the latest chemicals and processes on offer, even when dyeing period costumes.

Leaving the Dark Ages

I'm sometimes asked why I always use modern synthetic dyes. I would love to use natural dyes from medieval times but a) they wouldn't last and b) they are not actually healthier for you than modern substances – they used terrible things back then. And sometimes even innocuous ingredients can be dangerous when mixed with others. I've only been asked to dye something in natural dye once – and the result just wasn't as good.

— Liz Honeybone, Head Textile Artist

The textile studio plays a key role in creating uniquely patterned, coloured and textured fabrics for more fantastical costumes. For the theatre's 2017 production of *Saint George and the Dragon*, for instance, they came up with a remarkable design for the dragon's waistcoat, made by stencilling a pattern, scanning it multiple times and then printing it in different mediums. What emerged was a dark, reptilian fabric that resembled a shed snakeskin.

But even the less fantastical costumes often need work: it's rare that a production makes it on to the stage without calling on the textile studio at some point. The department might go to great lengths to get the exact right shade of mud for a uniform worn by a soldier fighting in the First World War in France, for instance. Contemporary outfits often need breaking down a bit to make them look as though they have been worn; some even need to look really battered and broken. Just the subtlest change in the appearance of a fabric can play a role in suggesting character.

A journey through the Costume department takes you on the journey of a costume: via meeting rooms, fitting rooms, storage cupboards, through the busy workroom, past tailors' dummies, racks of clothes, stacks of shoes and boxes of accessories, past the textile studio, the laundry with its rows of churning washing machines, and the drying room. It's a reminder that, when an actor steps onto the stage dressed as Henry V or Alice in Wonderland or Willy Loman, a huge amount of planning, invention and hard work has gone into making them look the part.

Hot plates, toupée tape and quick changes

For most of us, getting dressed plays a small part in our daily routine and laundry is just one task on our to-do list. For the Running Wardrobe department, it is a full-time job.

Once a show has made it onto the stage, costumes become the responsibility of the Wardrobe team, some 15 to 20 people (depending on the size of the shows in the repertoire) under the leadership of the wardrobe manager. Each show has several dressers, whose job is to make sure that the costumes are ready every show, deliver them to the

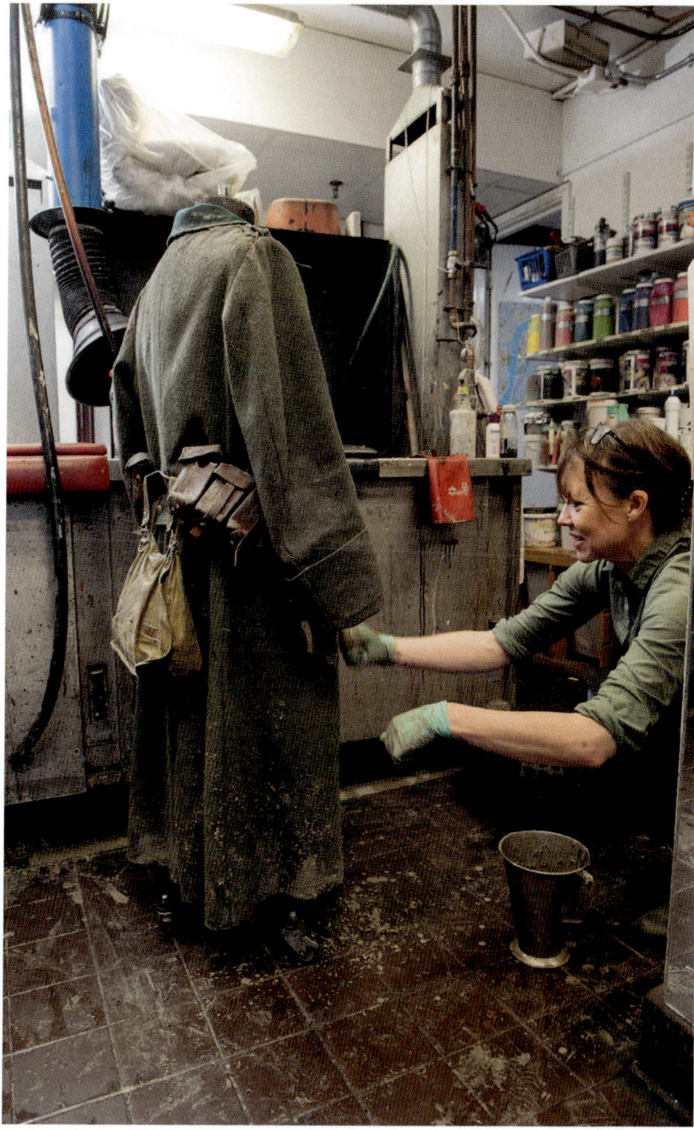

A textile artist making a uniform from *War Horse* look like it has seen battle

actors in their dressing rooms and check that outfits are available at the right time in the right place for quick changes.

Each of the three theatres has a hub where the dressers are based. That's where they bring costumes back at the end of the show for maintenance, repairs and cleaning, and where they collect them again before the next performance to deliver them to the cast.

Every dresser writes a 'track', or plot, of their responsibilities throughout the show and their journey: how they go from one change to another, one location backstage to another and what they have to collect and take to different spaces backstage.

One of the most crucial aspects of the dresser's role is to manage the 'quick changes': moments when an actor has to swap costumes in the wings mid-performance, often in the twinkling of an eye. For every show, the wardrobe department will establish a 'ladies' quick-change area' and a 'gent's quick-change area' – temporary spaces that are set up only for the duration of the production and that vary in position depending on the configuration of the backstage space. Frequently the dressers are working in the dark in a tiny area at the side of the stage with only a headlamp for illumination. The 'quick-change' is an art in itself and, like all arts, can sometimes reach extraordinary levels.

On the 2017 production of *Follies*, three dressers had less than one minute to change actor Peter Forbes, playing Buddy, out of a full suit – jacket, shirt, bow-tie, cummerbund, braces, trousers, socks, shoes – into another full suit. They used shirts that were split down the back, a bow-tie held on with Velcro and positioned one dresser at his front, one at his back and one solely working on his socks and shoes. The feet proved the most challenging: in the end they decided to put the actor's new socks on over his old ones because, although it's much easier to strip off a pair of socks to reveal the new ones underneath, there was too great a danger of ripping both sets off by mistake and so losing precious seconds.

The art of the quick change

The key to the quick change is organisation. You lay things out in particular order – in the order they are going on. So you'd start with a shirt, with the tie loosely tied under the collar, so it can go straight over the actor's head; you have trousers with all the fastenings open; shoes with the laces undone or tricked with elastic. You might do 'puddling': that's when you put a pair of trousers or skirt over the top of a pair of shoes so the actor steps straight into the pair of shoes and pulls the skirt or trousers up.

We choreograph the changes in detail – every time we do a change everything happens in the same way and it becomes automatic. Sometimes we'll have two members of the Wardrobe team on it, plus someone from Wigs, Hair and Make-up and someone from the Sound department plugging a mic in or something. They'll all be crammed in a space about a metre and a half square, behind the wing. We're in the dark, we can't speak loudly, and the clock is ticking. That's when the adrenalin kicks in!

In 2008 we did a production of Peter Handke's play *The Hour We Knew Nothing of Each Other*. It involved 450 different characters crossing a town square, played by 27 actors. There was somebody changing costume about every nine seconds throughout the evening. An actor would put something on at one side of the stage, walk across and come off at the other side, take the costume off and come back on in something else.

It was absolutely frantic. We had piles of costume at the side of the stage. We had teams of people standing either side, changing the actors, and we had other people taking away rails of costumes that were finished with and bringing in more. If you got it out of sequence, there was nowhere to go. I think once or twice something went wrong – like a hat or pair of shoes hadn't made it back to the right spot, but considering the scale of the thing, it went surprisingly well. The show itself was about an hour and 15 minutes long but it would take about two hours to set up for it and about two hours to unravel it all at the end.

— Michael Roff, Head of Running Wardrobe

The dressers also play a key part in realising changes of state for a character. An actor might go off in one scene and return in the next having been in a downpour, an accident or a fight, for example. Getting wet is generally achieved by using a garden spray: dressers gently mist the actor's hair and face, as if they were a thirsty house plant on a hot day. But if the actor is wearing a dark-blue coat, a simple misting might not be enough – any dampness will just vanish under the stage lights. Dressers might have to add a little glycerine to the water to make it stand on the surface of the garment. And sometimes mere moistness won't do – a character might have to be drenched. In such cases there is nothing for it but for the team to douse the lucky actor completely by tipping a tray of water over them – though they do thoughtfully ensure that the water is warm.

Maintenance is another key part of the Wardrobe department's role. The quick-change spaces are equipped with scissors, pins, threads, toupée tape (double-sided sticky tape used to keep wigs and hairpieces in place) – everything you might need to carry out running repairs for actors who have split their trousers, laddered their tights or ripped their robes. Often there is almost as much activity backstage as there is out front, with dressers running back and forth, stitching up a hole in the knee or finding a replacement for a mislaid item.

The staging of *Follies* called for specialist repairs: the exquisite feathery headdresses created by the Costume Props team and worn by the phantom showgirls were so delicate that bits would break off and they would also need frequent steaming to get them back into shape. The dancers' tap shoes required regular coatings of liquid rosin to prevent anyone skidding around on stage.

Meanwhile you'd often find a member of wardrobe lurking backstage with a tiny frying pan and a hotplate. This wasn't a ruse to cook supper during Act 2. The dancers' shimmering outfits were covered in thousands of tiny crystals, which fell off from time to time meaning the new ones had to be applied. The method for this is known as 'hot-stoning': the crystals came with heat-activated glue on the back of them, so a dresser would gently warm them in the frying pan until the glue softened, then stick them onto the fabric with a pair of tweezers.

Keeping things clean is also very important. All linen and underpinnings are freshly laundered for every show and costumes are regularly cleaned. That calls for a lot of soap and suds. There are 13 washing machines in the theatre, including one in each wardrobe 'hub', ranging from small domestic appliances to industrial top-loaders, and the laundry is equipped with huge packs of detergent.

The theatre also uses an ozone cabinet: a big, stainless steel box which contains a very strong amount of ozone. The ozone kills all the bacteria in the fibres of the cloth, removing any odours. This ingenious device enables dressers to clean up a costume without washing out any textural effects. If you have spent ages getting the mud down the side of a soldier's uniform correct, so it looks as though he has fallen off his horse, you don't want to have to send it to the dry-cleaners, lose all the mud, and have to paint it all back on. Pop it in the ozone cabinet, however, and the mud will stay intact, but any odours will be destroyed.

From the correct buttons on a costume, to the quickest technique for taking it off and the best strategy for cleaning it, the drive of both Costume and Wardrobe departments is to clothe a character in a way that supports the actor, convinces the audience and helps tell the story.

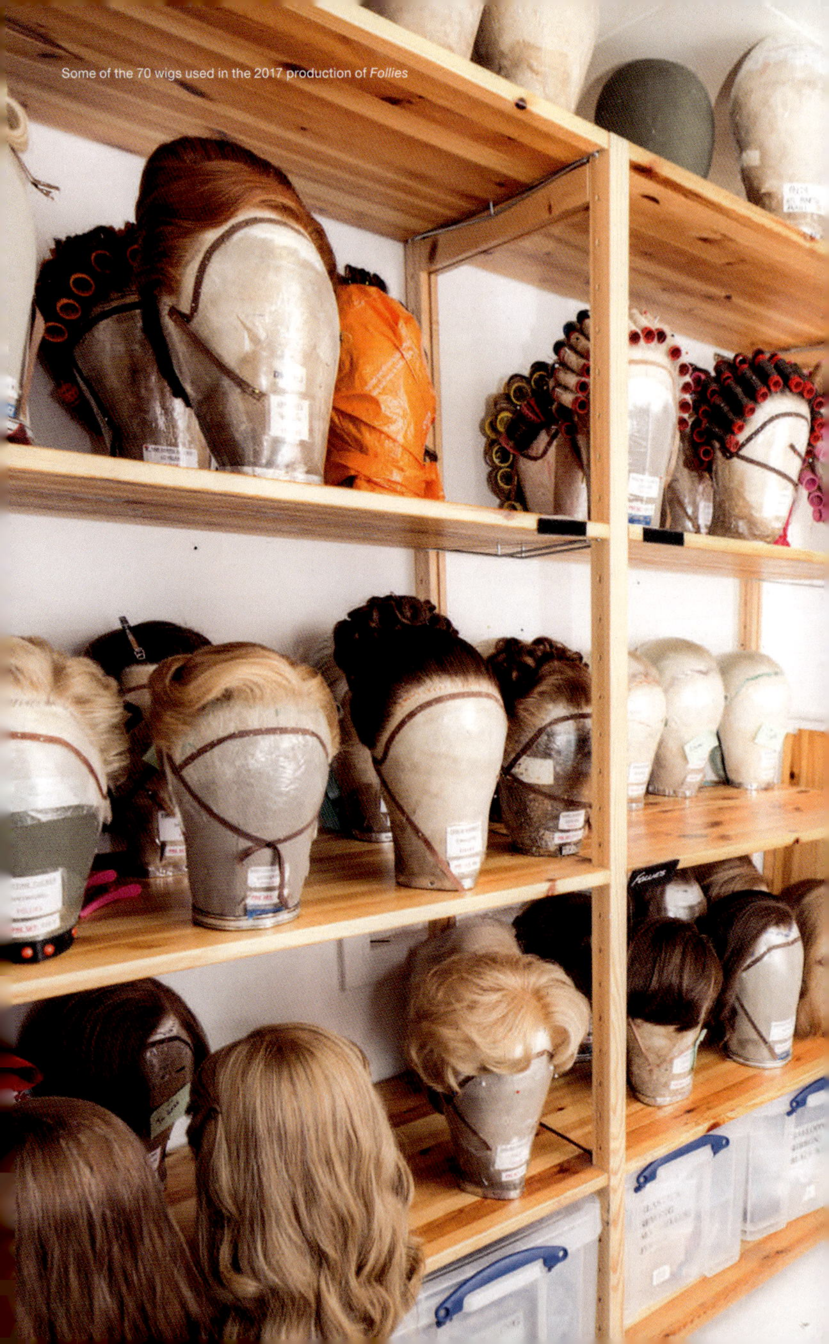

Some of the 70 wigs used in the 2017 production of *Follies*

13. Wigs, Hair and Make-Up

Keeping your hair on

We've all seen comic films in which the hero's attempt to disguise himself comes unstuck when his wig flies off or his moustache drops into his soup. It can be very funny when it happens deliberately in a comedy – it would be a disaster if it happened in the middle of *Macbeth*. It's part of the job of the Wigs, Hair and Make-up department to avoid such calamities.

WHAM, as the department is known in the building, is in charge of everything to do with an actor's appearance that doesn't come under costume: from gentle hairstyling to outrageous wigs; from subtle make-up to livid scars and oozing blood. They create all this in a bright, bustling room full of mirrors, wig stands, pins, scissors and hair-spray. Trolleys loaded with curlers and flexi-rods line the aisles. Drop into the department and you might find one person prepping a wig for that night's show, another experimenting with ghoulish wound techniques and a third painstakingly building a new wig.

Every wig is hand-made, each hair individually threaded through a mesh and knotted. The range and use of wigs varies enormously from tiny, naturalistic hairpieces to extravagant period coiffure.

A perfect head of hair

An average wig will cost between £1,500 and £2,000, use 100–150 grams of real human hair and take between 40 and 50 hours to make. I have very high standards about where the hair comes from: it must be ethically sourced. Hair tends to differ physically according to the region it is from. In southern European countries the hair is quite lush and strong – north European hair tends to be too thin and doesn't cope as well with colour. We started to use Indian hair but the structure is different – European hair has got a round shaft while Asian hair is flat so has a completely different texture.

We make the wigs on malleable blocks, padded to be a more exact replica of the actor's head. To get the shape accurate, we put a cling-film wrap around the actor's head, cover it in sellotape to keep the shape and then remove the mould. We then transfer that onto the block and build what we call a foundation.
A foundation is made of a very thin layer of lace – a tulle with holes – which we then cover with hair. You cover it completely with a mesh, thicker darker hair at back of head to keep the shape, then thinner at the front so it can disappear into the face of the actor. That is the structure of a wig. You then knot the hairs one by one in order to complete the wig. At the front you need to be very precise because that is where you are creating the hairline.

The majority of our work is trying to recreate a realistic head of hair. The best compliment you can give me is to believe there are no wigs on stage.

— Giuseppe Cannas, Head of Wigs, Hair and Make-up

The department's work varies enormously depending on both the play and the theatre: in the Dorfman the audience is much closer to the actors, so the work needs to be more subtle than for the larger Olivier, where more theatricality is called for. On many productions, decisions about wigs and hair tend to come quite late in the design process, so the time is often tight. Even so, WHAM never buys in wigs: every hairpiece worn on the theatre's three stages is made in the department. For a big historical work or a huge musical such as *Follies* (which called for 70 wigs in total), the department will often have to expand temporarily from its 12 full-time members of staff up to as many as 25.

With period pieces, accuracy is important. While the internet is a big help for research, it can also be deceptive – often the first images that come up on an internet search will be replica versions of period wigs and hairstyles created for films. It's important to dig more deeply if you want to find pictures and descriptions of the real thing.

It's easy to see the impact of the department on a production like *Amadeus*, set in 18th-century Vienna, but WHAM has a more invisible hand in nearly all shows. Many contemporary dramas also call for wigs, sometimes to facilitate quick changes: it is far quicker to swap a wig than to restyle a performer's hair. Even preparing a hairstyle pre-show might call for lengthy treatment with rollers, hairspray and other cosmetic products – not possible in the time available during a performance. Any chemical treatment that might be needed to style the hair every night could take a toll on it. And of course an actor's hair can alter substantially over the course of a long running show – grow, change style, even fall out – while the character's appearance needs to remain the same. Besides, actors don't always want to take the character home with them: if you have been playing a murderer, your hairstyle might make you see that murderer in the bathroom mirror when you get home. Wigs head off all these potential issues.

The department houses many sleek heads of hair, ready and waiting for their character to walk back out onto the stage. Meanwhile stock that can be reused is catalogued by length, type, colour and head size, and stored in drawers. There are several thousand wigs in storage.

Once the wigs are made, it is also the department's responsibility to fit them and maintain them. In between shows the wigs are reset and redressed then put in a hot room for a couple of hours to dry. And before and during the performance, members of WHAM will be working with actors to fit and adjust hair, wigs and make-up. As with costume dressers, they can find themselves working in tiny dark spaces backstage when they need to change things during the show. As Giuseppe Cannas, Head of Wigs, Hair and Make-up puts it, 'You have to be calm. You have to be organised. Equipment cannot move from place to place because you want to work on automatic pilot. You have to have firm nerves. If you panic, nothing will get done. If something has gone wrong, in my experience, time stops – so while everything is moving super-fast around you, you are moving at a pace that feels very slow. You go into a zone. If you breathe in the chaos, you will panic.'

But it is not just hair that can get hairy. WHAM also specialises in burns, wounds, scars, vomit and gore – pretty much anything that can happen to a body. The aim is to injure characters in as authentic a manner as possible without leaving so much as a scratch on the actor. At the far end of the workroom is a separate laboratory space where artists work on this task. There's an extractor vent above the desk and an array of cabinets in which flammables, solvents and chemicals are kept safely shut away.

It can be macabre work at times: for a production of *Macbeth* (2018), for instance, they had to try and replicate severed limbs using glycerine and food-colouring. 'If somebody faints, which they occasionally do, then you know you have done a good job,' says Cannas.

Sometimes simple household materials are the best – a tiny drop of washing-up detergent in fake blood can make it run smoothly and help to avoid staining. At other times the latest technology is required. When the theatre staged *Frankenstein* in 2011, the large scar across the creature's head was created using wax. But that older technique would have been too cumbersome for the more recent production, *Ugly Lies the Bone* by Lindsey Ferrentino (2017), in which a female veteran was struggling to recover from battle injuries and had burns across a great deal of her body. On film, make-up artists might have had five hours to create the effect, but in theatre they have at most an hour, so they deployed new silicon moulds.

Blood effects too can be challenging, largely because if anything goes wrong you can't stop and re-do it, as on film, and neither can you edit the action. On film, canny editing can produce the effects of a shooting or an accident, but on stage it all has to be executed live and if a blood capsule fails to burst the whole scene can be ruined. Likewise, the aftermath often cannot be cleaned away before the next scene, so gory effects need to be safe. WHAM works closely with directors, fight directors and the Special Effects department to ensure that harmful events within the drama look convincingly violent but in fact proceed safely.

The type of stage blood used can vary enormously, depending on the incident: the department buys some and makes others. Most is made using sugar so that an actor can swallow it – particularly useful if you have to get punched in the mouth during a fracas. But it's not just gruesome effects that the department manages: they also provide the basic make-up that enables the actors' features to be clearly seen in the theatre. And they carry out subtler tasks, such as ageing. On the bigger stages, the years might be added to a face through lines and shadows to change the shape and contours. For a more intimate staging, such as in the Dorfman, the team would need to use more refined, delicate techniques such as crows' feet around the eyes and a little latex padding to give the appearance of a double chin.

And as with all elements of performance, the increasing use of National Theatre Live (when productions are filmed on stage and broadcast, live,

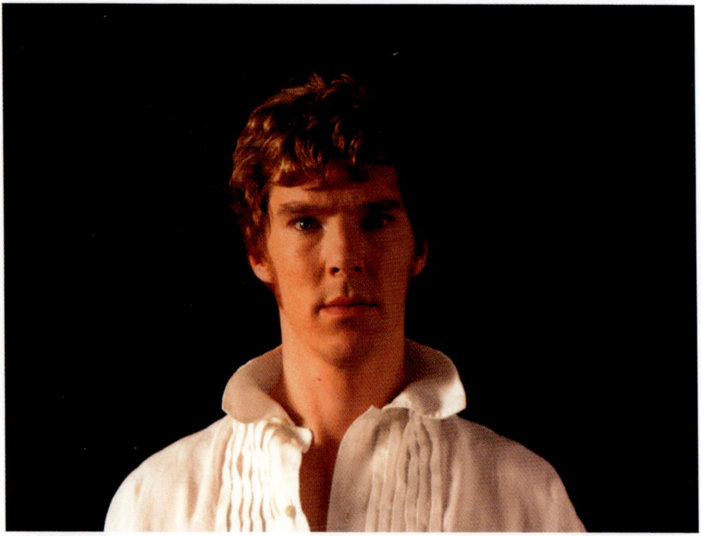

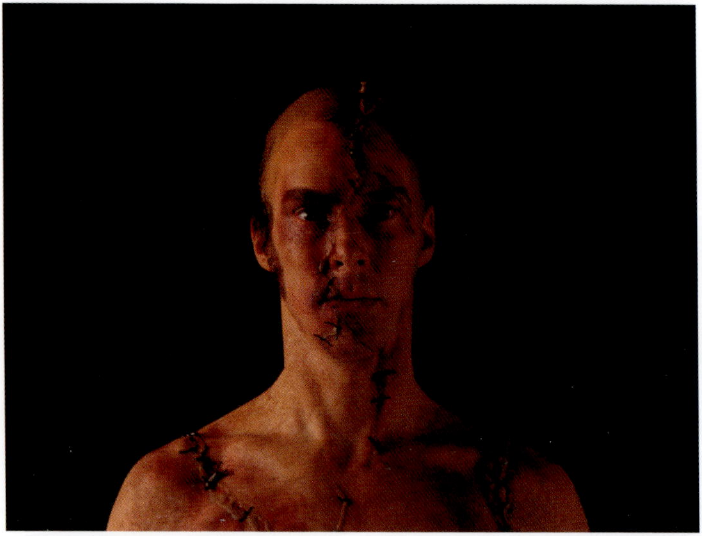

Benedict Cumberbatch as Victor Frankenstein (top) and the Creature (bottom) for *Frankenstein* (2011)

to cinemas around the world) has had an impact on the department. A broadcast calls for subtle differences to hair and make-up to accommodate close-ups and to ensure that an ageing technique, for instance, works for both the audience in the theatre and the audience in the cinema. The adjustments are often small – everyone is very clear that this is not a film but the live broadcast of a stage show. However, skin tones and hair colours sometimes read differently on camera. Microphones might need to be worked into a wig or the base of the wig might need to be better disguised.

We can all look old, tired or ill sometimes; we can all get wet in the rain or muddy in a fall. But those things happen to us by accident, often when we least want them to – characters on stage, on the other hand, require these effects on cue, and for that they need some help. In the Costume, Wardrobe and Wigs, Hair and Make-up departments, large numbers of people at the National spend their days doing just that: finding the best, most convincing way to age characters, beat them up, soak them in blood, rip their clothes to shreds and scar their faces – and then send the actors playing them home looking just as hale and hearty as they did when they arrived in the building.

Carly Bawden and Lois Chimimba in *wonder.land* (2015)

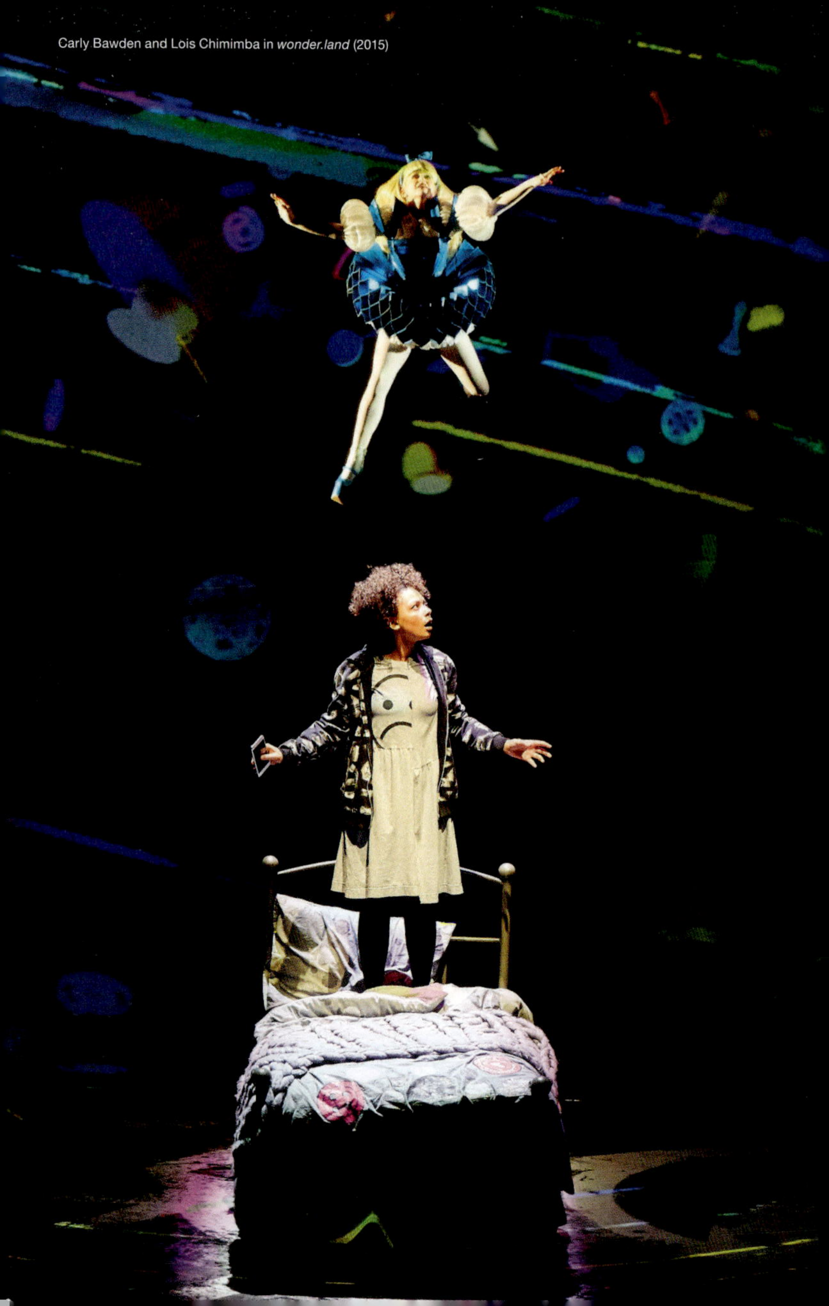

14. Lighting, Sound and Video

Let there be lighting

In Shakespeare's day, stage lighting was mostly down to nature: theatre companies scanned the skies and hoped that the sun would break through enough to illuminate the drama on their open-air stage. Then indoor theatres brought with them the need for illumination (just candles to begin with) and the first possibilities of experimenting with light and dark. Today, lighting plays a huge role in theatre: anyone who has ever been at a show when the lighting has failed will know just how critical it can be, not only in focusing the action, sculpting the space and shaping the mood, but even in the act of storytelling itself.

The National Theatre has some 3,000 stage lights in the building: hundreds in each auditorium, plus hundreds of extra options in storage for lighting designers to play with and for additional events, such as outdoor shows or press conferences. The Lighting team handles the installation, preparation and running of lighting designs in all three theatres, but they are also responsible for the maintenance and upkeep of the lighting stock, keeping the lights in good working order and staying abreast of advances in technology.

The idiosyncratic nature of the three theatres means that each stage brings attendant problems when it comes to lighting. The lighting technicians try to meet these challenges without losing the unique character of each auditorium.

The Olivier is a particularly tricky space to light: it has no proscenium arch and is so voluminous that it just seems to absorb light. (This theatre, of course, was inspired by the great open-air theatre in Epidaurus where the positioning and efficacy of stage lights was never a problem.) The Olivier stage needs particularly powerful lights and has a basic lighting rig of 600 units.

In the Lyttelton it is the unusual width of the stage that can cause headaches. And in the Dorfman, any problems are down to the theatre's flexibility. The old Cottesloe was so packed with its basic lighting rig that there was very little room for lighting designers to bring in their own ideas. When the space was refurbished and turned into the Dorfman, all that was ripped out and replaced by a number of 'intelligent' lights (which can be programmed to move). Now it can easily be lit in every configuration: end-on, in-the-round, and in traverse – though designers always have to be careful that a shaft of light on a performer won't end up illuminating part of the audience as well.

The job of a lighting designer

Lighting design can tell stories as much as scenery, costumes, music, sound: you can choose to do a show in very simple, stripped-back aesthetic or you can be very, very complicated. We are all storytellers, we just have different means by which to join in and tell the story.

In a way, you are doing lots of different jobs. You are being an editor – the rhythm of change in the show is all about lighting. You're also about hearing (if you can't see actors clearly it is harder to understand what they are saying). And you're being a storyteller and a dramatist. So it's a really interesting mixture.

If we look at *War Horse* (2007), when the audience walked into the theatre, the lighting was muted and there was a very simple space – like a blank sheet of paper. But then the first character walked into the space and was illuminated as he opened the book. So the idea was of the book bringing the story and the light bringing the story. Then around him we conjured sound and light and there was the idea that you lit the space as if it was a landscape. So it was quite nostalgic and old fashioned: the colours were very warm and there was light coming from a long way away as though it was coming from behind clouds. You brought the foal into that space, so what you were saying to the audience was 'this is a shared space – a shared space where we do very simple, gentle things and ask your imagination to conjure the rest'.

You were allowing their imagination to be triggered by things like gentle colour, a little shaft of light and a horse made out of bits of wicker and stick. In the same way that the horse was simple and naïve our lighting was simple and naïve – it was a shared space for collective moments of imagination. Later, when we went into the First World War trenches, the light went from being distant and far away to being low and active in the space and much more in the audience's eyes. So you were trying to shock people into what the experience was like. There's a game you play with the audience about what the rules are and then you change the rules and it has a big impact.

A lot of the set designer's work is at the early stages of a show. Mine is a lighter touch at that stage but through the last few weeks of rehearsals I get more and more involved and then in the technical rehearsals it is constant. That's my timeline. Technical rehearsals and previews are my most intense period of work.

— Paule Constable, lighting designer

The lighting designer will be part of the initial talks at the beginning of the production but they then tend to take a back seat for a while, popping in and out of rehearsals to see how the show is evolving. Their input really steps up in the last week of rehearsals, when they are able to watch run-throughs of the play and begin to finalise their plans.

Once the lighting designer has a plan, the lighting supervisor will study it to see what is required. While many of the new LED lights and all of the moving lights can change colour, the older lights still have to have colour film fitted in order to change, so that has to be sourced and cut to size in preparation. The rig will do great deal but designers often want to put in their own bits of equipment and if the set incorporates a scenic roof over the stage they won't be able to use the rig above it. And while the theatres have those programmable lights that can be moved automatically, they also still use follow spots (spotlights moved by hand follow the actor they are illuminating around the stage) and they still deploy many traditional methods, with technicians physically refocusing lights up in the rig.

The whole process hits crunch time when the show moves into technical rehearsals – the period when all the elements of cast, set, costumes, sound and lighting finally come together on stage and are painstakingly adjusted (technical rehearsals can take several days, especially if a show has a particularly complex set). Once the show is up and running, the lighting team will have to change the setup every time the production goes into or out of the theatre repertoire. They notate and label every light, so that any that are changed or removed can be slotted quickly back in, and on changeover days, they start work at 8am to disassemble the rig for one show and set up the rig for the incoming show.

Some shows are, of course, more lighting-intensive than others. One of the most startling uses of lighting in the theatre's history occurred in Danny Boyle's 2011 staging of *Frankenstein* in the Olivier Theatre, with set design by Mark Tildesley and lighting design by Bruno Poet. The set design included a vast forest of hundreds of assorted sized lightbulbs hanging over the entire auditorium, each suspended by an individual cord. These lights were for much more than just effect: they formed part of the story telling process, encapsulating the narrative's interest in electricity and life. They would glow, pulse brighter and darker in the rhythm of a heart-beat, and sometimes flow into patterns. It was an ingenious and remarkable idea but a fiendish challenge for the Lighting department – every single light bulb had to have its own dimmer.

The popular stage adaptation of Mark Haddon's novel *The Curious Incident of the Dog in the Night-Time* (2012) likewise embedded the lighting design into the storytelling. Paule Constable's lighting, together with Finn Ross' video design, created pictures and patterns on the floor and walls of the set to allow for quick changes of scene, but also to envelope the audience in Christopher's intense world and help them to share his experience when his environment became too overwhelming. He hated the colour yellow, for instance, so whenever things became frightening, the lighting would turn yellow.

The right Light

Often doing something minimal is harder than having all the bells and whistles. Love (2016) by Alexander Zeldin was a good example – it was set in a sheltered accommodation hostel and needed flat, bland, utilitarian lighting. In plan form, it perhaps didn't feel like there was enough there, but actually any more would have been too much.

— Matt Drury, Head of Lighting

Every lighting designer has their own style and flair, just like any artist. Some are more traditional, some very stylised. There are innovations too: most recently LED tape has brought new possibilities into stage lighting: it can easily change colour, bend and twist, meaning that designers can use light to sculpt the space more effectively.

There are definite fashions in stage lighting, too. At one time everything was very strongly front-lit. Recently, the trend has been for lighting from the sides, back and top of the stage, which can be more subtle and sculptural. Having created a layered lighting look on the stage, the designer can then bring a little front light to bear in order to lift the actors' faces out of the image they have created. But however atmospheric or beautiful the lighting is, what is essential is that the audience can still see the performers. One of the curious but important rules of theatre is that if an audience can't see the actors clearly, they can't hear them. Which brings us on to…

Sound and video

When we consider sound in theatre we tend to think of effects – guns, thunderbolts and so on. But in fact the Sound and Video department's remit is wide-ranging, from simple audibility through to music and complex audio and visual effects. The sound of a door slamming or a distant gunshot might be crucial to the action of the narrative but ambient birdsong or traffic noises might also help to establish and support the setting. And increasingly theatre directors and sound designers use soundscapes as part of their armoury: carpets of music and sound that subtly create mood and tension and can work stealthily on an audience's emotions. A production of Shakespeare's *King Lear* might involve big sound effects to invoke the crucial storm on the heath, but it might also use music or carefully selected effects either between or underneath scenes to augment the atmosphere.

Sound effects can of course be generated live – the tinkle created by a character dropping a set of keys or the smashing of a pile of dishes can be made by someone doing exactly that in the wings near a microphone. Foley, named after sound effects artist Jack Foley and often used in radio broadcasting, are specially produced effects: walking a pair of boots on a tray of gravel to denote approaching footsteps; crumpling paper to represent a crackling fire; chopping a cabbage in half to suggest the grim noise of a head being hacked off.

The Sound and Video department at the National Theatre still use many of these traditional techniques. But they also make use of the increasingly sophisticated technology on offer. Some effects – a creaking inn sign, a hooting owl – are best recorded elsewhere and reproduced through the speakers and even simple noises can be recorded in advance to ensure that they have the same quality and impact every night.

The magic of Foley

The brilliance of Foley is that it takes a sound and, by removing the original visual context for it, completely transforms its meaning. If you watch someone crumpling some paper, you immediately pair the sight with the sound. But if you hear that same sound while you're looking at a fire on stage, you immediately pair it with that sight instead, and hear the noise of a crackling fire. It's satisfying because you are making use of the audience's imaginations without them even being aware it's happening.

— Dominic Bilkey, Head of Sound and Video

Locating sound is a complex job too. If you have a crying baby, a ringing telephone or a braying donkey on stage, you want the noise they make to appear to come from them, not from speakers that are metres away from them. The team will secrete tiny speakers onto them, (and if necessary onto characters or elements of set nearby) to give the desired impression. When 'Eggy Tom' brought on a talkative crow in DC Moore's *Common* (2017), the actor playing the character had several speakers concealed in her costume so that the bird's caws came from the right place and were audible at the back of the Olivier Theatre.

The department is also responsible for assisting actors themselves in being heard. This usually entails the use of tiny microphones, fixed to the actor's head and attached by a thin wire to a radio transmitter pack hidden in their costume. This pack in turn sends a signal to a central receiver, which sends it to the manually operated sound desk. From there it is sent to a processor, then to an amplifier, and finally to the speakers which distribute the sound through speakers around the theatre. Radio mics are not used on all productions – different styles of performance, the acoustics of a set design, or specific action on stage may affect whether or not mics are appropriate. Changing audience tastes are also a factor here: some styles of projection and enunciation heard in Victorian theatres might seem excessively mannered now, and mics can support a less formal style kind of performance.

Sound designers and members of the department attend early production meetings to establish the show's requirements. Some set designs affect audibility and, as with lighting, the theatres themselves present an array of challenges. A great deal of work has gone into making the acoustics work in the Olivier, for example. Although it looks like an amphitheatre, the acoustics are very different from those in an open-air space – it has soft surfaces that can absorb sound – so various amendments have been made over the years to reflect sound in some areas and dampen it in others. The Lyttelton's proportions – the very wide and high stage, for example – can create difficulties, while the Dorfman's flexibility means that the space tends to shapeshift, demanding different solutions in different configurations.

Then there are the demands of the show itself. If the cast need to wear radio mics what they have to do on stage may affect how they are deployed. The theatre's 2017 production of *Follies* used 56 radio mics: not only did the whole cast wear mics, but the dancers also had extra ones for their tap shoes, with wires running down their legs to just above their feet. The sound department had to balance all these with the music from the on-stage orchestra.

There are usually several members of the department assigned to each show, with some positioned backstage to affix or adjust mics during the performance – all of this done in cramped conditions in the dark, alongside the dressers and make-up assistants who may be working on an actor's costume and appearance. Vigorous action such as fighting can dislodge mics, while both water and nudity pose particular challenges. The answer is usually a discreet mic hidden in a wig – together with assurances that the actor in question will keep their head above water. Sand is also a problem because of its abrasive nature – scenes set on the beach tend not to be a favourite for the team.

The job of a sound designer

Sound design falls into two categories and I've been very lucky to do both. One is content, which is the creation of music, soundscapes, sound effects – things that you add a production to give it its character and make it what it is. The other side is delivery. Where the content has been created by someone else – the composer, for example – and your job is to make it happen.

How do you make the actors audible and how do you balance that with an orchestra or a band?

Content is very creative and delivery is very technical. I would say a knowledge of both is very important at the National Theatre because of the three theatres, one (the Dorfman) is acoustically excellent and allows you to be very flexible in your staging, and the other two are very difficult for acoustics, audibility and intelligibility.

There's a rule of air volume. In an ideal situation, there should be somewhere between two and a half and four cubic metres of air in the space per audience member – then everyone should be able hear what's happening on stage. In an opera house, there is between nine and a half and 12 cubic metres of space per audience member, so it's much more reverberant. In those wonderful Frank Matcham theatres [playhouses designed by the Victorian theatre architect] the average volume that each audience member enjoys is about 2.8 cubic metres, which is really small, which means there's very little wasted air for the actor to have to excite before the sound gets to the audience member. So Matcham houses work very well acoustically. The Olivier has a staggering 11.6 cubic meters of air around each person; that's an awful lot of space. So the sound designer's job in the Olivier includes helping to address the issues that creates.

There is also the issue of reflected sounds coming back off the walls which can be confusing to the ears. So even in areas of the auditorium where the level of sound is adequate, the intelligibility can still be affected. We've developed techniques so that most of time audience not aware of the use of mics, so that they aren't a barrier between the actor and the audience – we just use them to help direct the sound where it needs to go, assisting the acoustics of the room rather than making the actors voice louder.

Sound and music have a direct route to the emotions: they don't go through a registration process in the brain – you just feel something. That's what makes it so powerful. Sound in a play can also help give a sense of location, give you information about the weather, and it can even tell you what period you are in.

— Paul Arditti, sound designer

And, as the name suggests, the Sound and Video department also works closely with the Lighting department on in-show video, which is now often integral to a show. This was certainly the case with *wonder.land*, the 2015 update of *Alice in Wonderland*, in which an immersive video game became the wonderland. Digital technology blended with live performance to send giant images and avatars floating across the Olivier stage. It was spectacular but also crucial to the storytelling: if the projection went wrong the whole show would disintegrate.

Broadly speaking video is used in two ways. The first of these is narrative: video projections which are part of the story itself. The most impressive example of this in recent years was *Network* (2017). Set in a television news studio, it featured a huge video wall at the back of the set onto which the station's broadcasts were played. These were created live each night by two on-stage camera people (acting as the studio's camera men) and a video mixer. There was even a scene which was broadcast by wireless video link from outside on the South Bank every night.

The second use might be called environmental augmentation: using projections to create atmosphere or scenery in addition to the set. A good example of this was *Ugly Lies the Bone*, where the sweeping cityscape at the back of the set (described in Chapter 11) was brought to life by

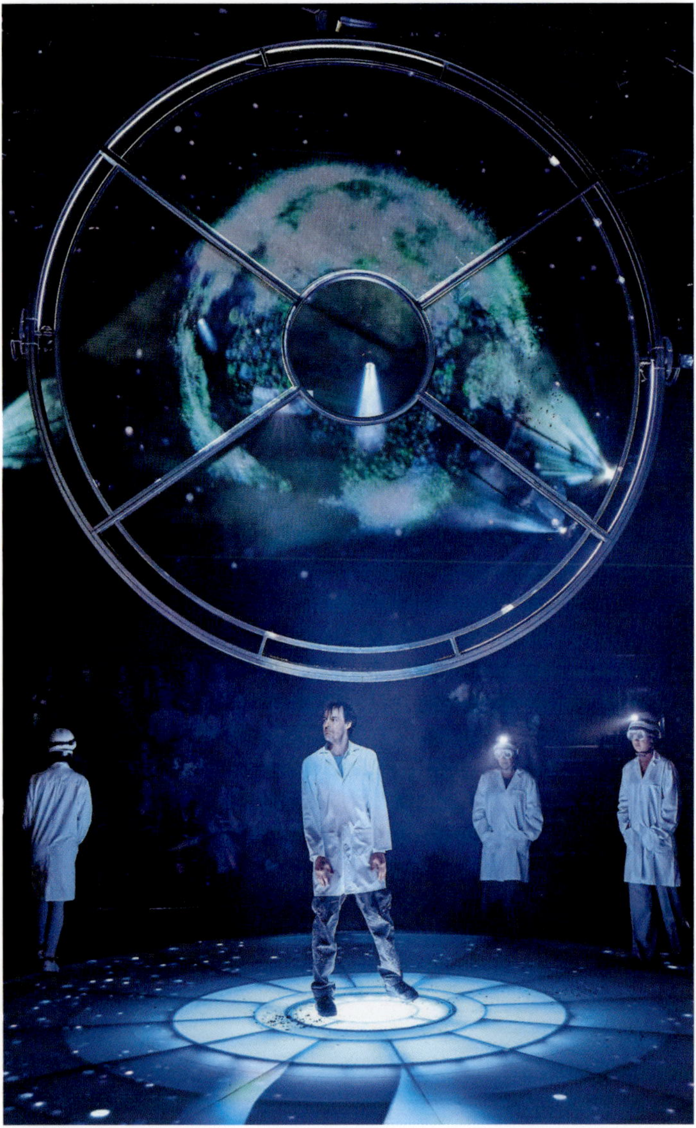

Paul Hilton and members of the *Mosquitoes* company (2017)

Luke Halls' video projections precisely mapped on to the plain shapes of the miniature buildings. At other points it became an enormous digital snowscape to represent the VR game which Jess, the main character, used to manage her severe pain. Similarly, in *Mosquitoes* (2017) video designer Ian William Galloway used swirling astronomical projections to echo explanations of physics that formed part of the play.

These two uses of video frequently combine, as in the *The Lehman Trilogy* (2018) where projections, designed once again by Luke Halls, helped to redefine the spartan office space that formed the set as the cotton fields of Alabama or the New York cityscape, but advanced the action of the plot at the same time – by showing those same cotton fields ablaze, for example.

As new technologies become available the Sound and Video department is able to create ever more complex audio-visual effects, helping writers and directors to tell stories in new and more ambitious ways.

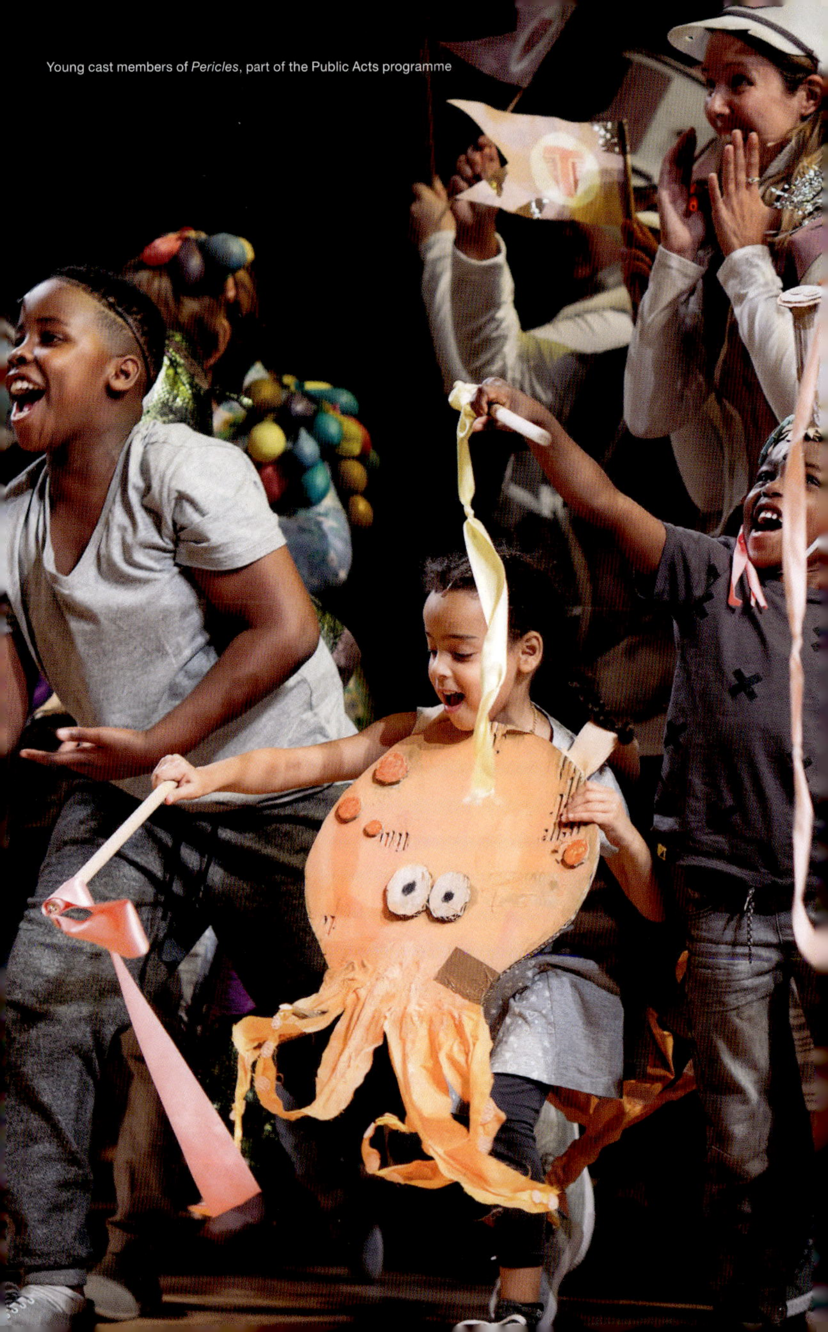

Young cast members of *Pericles*, part of the Public Acts programme

15.

Building Links and Looking to the Future

Most of what happens in the National Theatre is about the here and now: the work that is playing on the stages every night. But there's also a drive to expand beyond that: to reach people who can't physically attend the shows by using live broadcasts; to open up opportunities for audiences to engage with artists and ideas through talks, exhibitions and events; to preserve the work for future generations; and to move towards that future by experimenting with new forms and by encouraging young artists and audiences.

Preserving the past: the National Theatre Archive

The National Theatre as a building is solid and durable; the work that defines it, however, is not. One of the great qualities of live theatre is that it is transient. Productions differ subtly even from night to night and once a show has finished, it is gone. It's what makes being in an audience so special, but it also means that even the greatest performances can vanish into thin air. That's where the National Theatre Archive comes into play.

The Archive, housed in the same building as the Studio, is a remarkable institution packed with details about every show ever staged by the theatre since Peter O'Toole walked on at the Old Vic for the opening of *Hamlet* in 1963. The Archive's aim is to document, preserve and make accessible everything related to the National Theatre – from the campaigns to found it, going back to the 19th century, to the latest developments happening today.

It's all free to access, whether you are a professional theatre-maker, an academic, a student or just a curious member of the public. You can make an appointment and sit in the research room, poring over programme notes and books of your choice, or watch one of the hundreds of recordings of productions in a screening room (either individually or in groups of up to 70). It's an invaluable resource, connecting the current work at the NT with all the drama and debate that has gone on throughout its life.

In the high-capacity rolling shelves in the Archive storeroom are boxes dedicated to every production ever mounted. Each one is a little treasure chest of memorabilia: photos from the rehearsals and the show; programmes; press cuttings; prompt scripts with all the rehearsal notes and the blocking and cuing; costume bibles with all the costume details, designs and swatches of material; and the stage management reports from every performance.

The box from the National Theatre's opening production of *Hamlet* includes telegrams wishing the company luck. One message, making a pun on a speech from the play, reads 'MAY YOU BE THE VERY BUTTON OF FORTUNE'S CAP TONIGHT, FROM JOHN AND JOHN.' The collection from *Rosencrantz and Guildenstern Are Dead*, from 1967, includes details of the production's tour to Broadway (it was the first NT show to visit New York), such as a wonderful photograph of someone selling coffee to the ticket queue. Put together with video footage (all productions since 1995 have been video recorded, including those not filmed for National Theatre Live) and recordings and notes of all Platform events (public talks and discussions about the production or the themes raised), these physical souvenirs offer a vivid and detailed record of the production, long after it has gone.

The practice of filming all the productions also makes for an important educational resource: if you are studying *King Lear*, even if the NT doesn't have it on stage you can come to the Archive and compare and contrast four productions of that play that it has staged in the past.

As well as the cultural archive, which holds everything relating to the shows and the artistic life of the National Theatre, the building houses the business archive and several external collections. The former contains everything to do with the running of the theatre: masterplans of the building, evaluations, feedback, and even minutes from the heated committee meetings at which the design of the theatres was decided.

The external collections, meanwhile, are items donated by other people, often former staff members and artists. By far the biggest of these is the Jocelyn Herbert collection – objects, drawings and notebooks relating to the great, highly influential designer.

There are over 6,000 drawings of Herbert's set and costume designs, all of which are beautiful items in themselves. Herbert seems to have been incapable of producing a boring, functional sketch – her images are lively and vivid, the figures have clear facial expressions, some of them mischievous, others worried. A sketch of a toga for *Julius Caesar* includes instructions to the wardrobe assistant on how to drape it and some cheeky anatomical details.

The Archive also houses the masks Herbert designed for Peter Hall's ground-breaking production of *The Oresteia*: contained in boxes on the shelves, they are slightly sinister objects with their sightless eyes and gaping mouths. And then there are 400 of her notebooks from when she was 16 through to the day she died, which are wonderfully eclectic, including sketches and designs alongside shopping lists, draft letters and personal notes such as 'wash hair'.

The Archive has also collaborated with the Black Cultural Archives, Sustained Theatre and Arts, and Arts Council England to create the Black Plays Archive, which documents the first professional production in the UK of any play written by a black British, African or Caribbean playwright, telling you where it was staged, who wrote it, who was in it, naming the production team and, importantly, explaining where you can go to find out more. In time this important resource will play its part in making such work better known and getting it on to school and university syllabuses.

Digital access plays an increasing part in making the Archive available to people who can't visit it in person. Meanwhile, although much of the material is kept in the building, several hundred boxes are kept in the DeepStore archive: a unique storage space housed in a vast salt mine in Cheshire that stretches to the size of 700 football pitches and houses over two and a half million documents for institutions such as the police and the National Health Service. It is a perfect facility for keeping documents as it is dry, extremely secure and there is no UV light. This dark, underground facility makes an extraordinary dormitory for the live, public art form that is theatre.

Nurturing the future: learning and participation

There's an early black and white photograph from the 1970s of excited primary school children standing in a neatly snaking queue outside the new National Theatre. They, like the building at that time, are at the beginning of their lives – and they are among the first of thousands and thousands of young people who will go on to pass through the doors of the theatre and engage with live drama.

From the very outset, the National Theatre aspired to be an open and welcoming space for young people. But in the decades since that early photograph was taken, the theatre's work in reaching out to children, school-pupils, students, families and communities has grown exponentially. The Learning department now has a huge remit, driven by the principle that a National Theatre should bring theatre to the widest possible audience, should stimulate creativity and should lead by example. 'We've got a responsibility to the health of the theatre sector,' explains Alice King-Farlow, Director of Learning. 'And the health of the theatre sector partly depends on people encountering theatre at a young enough age to get involved. We take that responsibility seriously.'

On the ground, that task translates into a large number of rolling programmes: some are focused on watching theatre, others on making it; some are based in the building on the South Bank, others head out on the road to visit schools and colleges around the country.

Perhaps the most prominent of them all is the Connections festival: an annual and uplifting event that encourages thousands of secondary schools and youth theatres across the nation to participate, each choosing to perform one of a set of purpose-written new plays by renowned playwrights.

Since it started in 1995, Connections has commissioned more than 160 brand new plays by leading playwrights – including James Graham, Jackie Kay, Bryony Lavery, Patrick Marber, Mark Ravenhill and Philip Ridley, building an entirely new repertoire of plays for young performers.

Around 300 youth theatre or school theatre groups take part in Connections each year. The director of each participating group attends a development weekend at the National Theatre, working with the playwrights and with NT practitioners, before returning to their school or youth group to begin rehearsals. And each group performs at least twice: once in their own venue and once on the stage of one of around 30 partner theatres around the country, leading professional theatres that host a festival for Connections companies in their area. The year finishes with a festival at the National Theatre itself: an inspiring annual event which sees the Dorfman taken over for a full week by 13–19-year-olds from across the UK.

Participants learn not just to act, but to direct, design, light and stage manage shows. Many of those who take part go on to find work in the arts, both on stage and backstage. Others will go on to become not the performers but the audiences of the future. And for many, the experience is simply an eye-opener to what theatre can do: how moving, funny or illuminating it can be. With arts education under increasing pressure in schools, Connections makes a high-profile and practical commitment to the value of theatre and the role it can play in education and personal development. Participants acquire life-skills such as learning to speak in public, solve problems, meet deadlines and work collaboratively. And the rehearsal room is a democratic place where everyday school hierarchies can be forgotten and ideas explored in a safe environment. For many young people, taking part can make a sizeable personal impact.

Let's Play, introduced more recently, provides a similar opportunity for even younger students. Directed at primary schools (ages 4–11), it offers these younger pupils and their teachers a chance to have a go at staging a new, specially commissioned drama by an experienced playwright. Teachers attend a two-day course in theatre-making, led by professionals, and then head back to their schools to work with their youthful students on performing the play they have chosen.

'It's an explicit invitation to schools,' says King-Farlow. 'We're saying, "Here's a new play you can do with your school: it's really lively, with great songs, it's designed for big classes to perform, it encourages children to get involved in every aspect of theatre-making – design, stage management, writing and performing." And the programme gives a lot of support about how to run rehearsals, vocal warm-ups and all the sort of things that you don't necessarily know if you're not a specialist drama teacher. There's also another aim to it which is about demonstrating how theatre can work with the curriculum – so each of the plays comes with curriculum resources around it, so schools can connect the work on the play across to other teaching.'

The National also sends out regular tours of Shakespeare plays, specially adapted for primary schools (cut down to an hour and performed by a group of just eight actors), offering a chance for under-11s to discover and enjoy Shakespeare and experience his work as live drama, rather than as simply a text to study. And then there are *Make Theatre* days in the NT's Clore Learning Centre, which provide classes with a tour of the building tailored to primary school children and a workshop on one particular aspect of theatre-making.

'We're really interested in young people getting access to the technical and backstage aspects of theatre because those are the least well-known,' explains King-Farlow.

That hands-on, practical streak also characterises much of the output for secondary school pupils and young people. The Clore Learning Centre is home to the Young People's Programme for 16–21-year-olds, which offers workshops and courses on everything from producing to special effects and make-up, and to the Young Technicians Programme for 14–18-year-olds.

The NT runs tours to secondary schools, again of works adapted specifically for the task – including an adapted version of *The Curious Incident of the Dog in the Night-Time* which visited 60 schools across the UK in 2018; and runs extensive education programmes around its national tours. The theatre also shares performances digitally through *National Theatre: On Demand. In Schools* – schools can sign up and have free access in the classroom to a number of National Theatre Live recordings, together with background educational resources – and runs numerous conferences and events. A 2017 conference on *Macbeth* brought 700 secondary school students to the theatre.

'Our events help students understand that a play is more than a text on the page,' explains King-Farlow. 'We're constantly trying to demonstrate that the words on the page are a blueprint – to be reinterpreted each time by a collaborative team of actors, director and designer and many others and set in a world that has to be invented and imagined and made for each production. So we usually demonstrate some aspect of that process – for instance, taking a scene and working through from first reading to the final staged version. There are usually some moments for students to come up on stage and try things out and we aim to give students the chance to hear from core members of the production team team.'

Another exciting strand of the National's work for schools is New Views: a programme that invites students aged 14–19 to write their own plays. Again, teachers attend a weekend of advice and guidance with professional writers (a workshop on research, for example, or on creating character or structure and endings), then return to their schools to run a playwriting group with students, usually outside curriculum time. Later a team of playwrights visit the schools twice – once to run workshops with the students and help stimulate ideas, once for one-to-one sessions with each of the students on the script they have started writing. Eventually the students submit half-hour scripts to the National Theatre – from around 300 scripts submitted, a team of readers from across the NT select a shortlist of ten.

'We hold a New Views festival each year and give rehearsed readings with professional actors to all the shortlisted plays. And we pick one winning play and give it a fully professional production,' says King-Farlow. 'So one young writer aged between 15 and 19 every year gets their play performed at the National Theatre for three performances.'

At the heart of all these initiatives is a core aim to open up the National Theatre to the widest possible range of ages, backgrounds and enthusiasms and to make both theatre-going and theatre-making feel accessible to anyone. Talks, debates, workshops and exhibitions aim to expand on the NT's repertoire, offering insights into the processes of making a show and expanding on the themes addressed in the plays.

A talk to accompany *Hadestown* (Anaïs Mitchell and Rachel Chavkin's musical about Orpheus and Eurydice), for example, discussed the enduring fascination of ancient myths; an event about the epic play, *The Lehman Trilogy,* brought the three actors – Simon Russell Beale, Adam Godley and Ben Miles – to the stage to discuss with the audience how they made the show. When the theatre staged Brian Friel's *Translations* in 2018, there were events exploring Irish history; in 2018 an exhibition celebrated 100 years of women having the vote alongside a series of rehearsed readings celebrating the fight for political equality. Meanwhile regular backstage tours open up the building, allowing the public to get a glimpse of what goes on behind the scenes, while hands-on experiences offer a chance to watch, perform and create theatre.

Public Acts

One of the most recent and striking examples of the National Theatre's principles of inclusivity is Public Acts, an initiative to create extraordinary acts of theatre and community. The first Public Acts production was *Pericles*, in a new adaptation by Chris Bush with music by Jim Fortune, directed by Emily Lim. Performed over three nights in the Olivier in 2018, it brought over 200 members of the public onto the huge stage as performers. A community company of 120 were drawn from eight community partners across London, joined by cameo performance groups including choirs, dance crews, a cheerleading squad and musicians, showcasing the cultural diversity of London.

Pericles was a landmark event for the National Theatre – 'What is a national theatre for?' asked *The Times* review – 'The answer was defiantly this: inclusive, empowering, revitalising, celebratory, multicultural, multilingual and downright fun'. *As You Like It* followed in 2019 at the Queen's Theatre Hornchurch, working with the same eight community partners and future plans will see further Public Acts productions in partnership with theatres and community organisations beyond London.

'The National aims to be a theatre for everyone and that should extend to performing and creating as well as watching theatre.' says Alice King-Farlow. 'And it's recognising that alongside our cultural mission we have a civic and a social responsibility.'

Expanding the present: National Theatre Live

When a show is a hit, there is nothing quite like sitting in the theatre, watching, live, with hundreds of other people around you. But what if you can't make it to the theatre? Perhaps it's sold out. Or you live hundreds – or even thousands – of miles away.

National Theatre Live is the response to that all too common frustration. Established in 2009, it's the practice of broadcasting performances, live, to cinemas worldwide. It was launched by David Sabel, with the encouragement of the NT's then-Director Nicholas Hytner, who had experienced live broadcasts of his work with the New York Metropolitan Opera and realised how much he would have relished such an opportunity when he was a theatre-hungry teenager.

The first transmission was Racine's *Phèdre*, in 2009, with Helen Mirren playing the title character. NT Live has gone on to broadcast dozens of productions – rising from four a year to 12–15 annually, from about 500 to 3,000 cinemas and from 20 territories to 65. That means millions of people have been able to watch National Theatre shows, plus some from other theatres: NT Live includes productions from companies other than the NT itself, and other broadcasts have included *A View from the Bridge*, with Mark Strong (from the Young Vic), *Macbeth*, with Kenneth Branagh (from Manchester International Festival) and *Hamlet* with Benedict Cumberbatch (from the Barbican Centre).

But isn't film a sworn rival to theatre? Doesn't filming productions have a negative impact on the number of people attending the actual show?

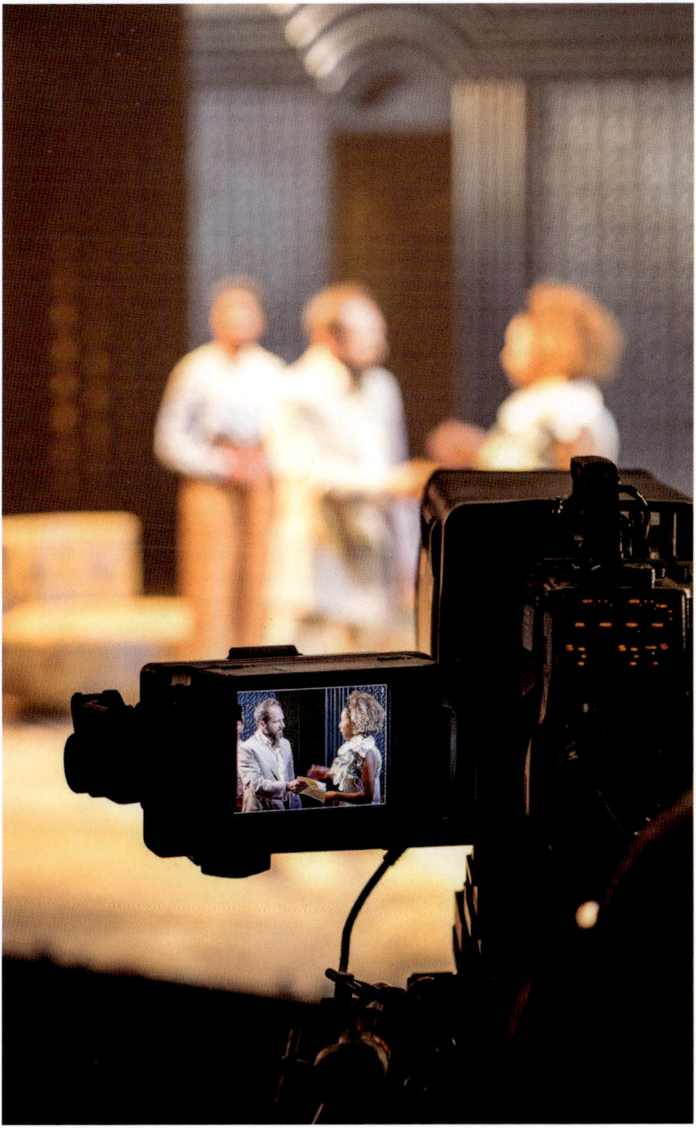

National Theatre Live filming of *Antony and Cleopatra* (2018)

Emma Keith, Head of NT Live, explains that quite the reverse has proved true. Theatre audience numbers have more than held up.

'It has absolutely gone the other way,' says Keith. 'Now we probably reach between 1 million and 1.5 million people worldwide through NT Live each year. We have, in a way, a limitless capacity in the cinema. We now offer the opportunity for encore screenings so we might be able to play a show five times. *Hamlet* with Benedict Cumberbatch reached an audience of over 800,000 people – there was no way that show was going to play in a theatre long enough to reach that number of people otherwise.'

Indeed, she adds, many people even visit shows twice – once in the cinema, once in the theatre. Meanwhile broadcasting to other countries – Australia, for instance – means that theatre-goers there have an opportunity to see the work of the National and so know what to expect when the company is able to visit those countries: 'We've done productions at the National that we have filmed and broadcast, they have then gone into the West End or to Broadway or on international tours having already been in the cinema and actually it just helps generate interest in the production itself.'

The main objection to filming theatre in the past has been the quality. Film and live theatre are very different media, so in the past stage productions, filmed often from the back of the stalls, tended to look stilted and remote. They could end up falling between two stools, offering neither the vibrant experience of being in the theatre nor the sophisticated realism of purpose-made film. NT Live set out to offer something much more bespoke, says Keith.

'When it started, Nicholas Hytner said, "If we're going to do this we're going to do it properly. We're going to create an experience that is designed to be had in cinemas." So we completely give over the auditorium to cameras, we give them the best seats in the house. We lose anywhere between 200 and 300 seats to accommodate them. We can have cameras on track, we can have them on a crane, we can have a tower camera that goes up and down, so that we can give the cinema audience the best experience possible. It's like watching a sports match on TV – it's not the same as being there in the stadium, but it is a very good and valid experience in its own right.'

There is no set way of filming a show: each production is assessed and handled according to what it needs to come across. But once the cameras are fixed and the show begins, the actors then proceed as they do in every other performance, playing to the audience in the theatre and forgetting that the filming is being done. The idea is to capture a live theatre performance as well as possible, not to tailor a performance to film. So there are no retakes, no sound-track added afterwards, no post-production edits. The production is broadcast exactly as it is – if something goes wrong, it stays wrong – even at later screenings. That liveness is key to the enterprise, as is the presence of the theatre audience. In fact, viewers who have seen shows in the cinema report a sense of affinity with their counterparts in the auditorium as both react to what is happening on stage.

Decisions about which shows are screened depend on the repertoire: the aim is to get a broad selection of drama and styles, reasonably spaced out over the year (rather than several all in one month). One drawback of advance planning is that, because the programming has to be done around six months in advance, it is not possible to respond immediately to a show that unexpectedly becomes a hit.

'There are things that sound amazing but don't turn out quite as we hoped,' says Keith. 'Others fly under the radar and then become big hits when they open and we feel we have missed an opportunity. There are always decisions to be made and times when we kick ourselves that we made the decision we did. But you live with it. That's theatre!'

The Immersive Storytelling Studio

One big question facing contemporary theatre-makers is whether to incorporate new technology into productions and, if so, how. The digital revolution has been so fast and so far-reaching – and is advancing so swiftly – that the National Theatre now has a whole department dedicated to exploring new technologies and their potential role in live theatre.

The Immersive Storytelling Studio is a space where artists – writers, directors, storytellers and theatre makers – can work alongside creative technologists.

The National Theatre's engagement with digital technology and virtual reality has increased over the years both on stage and front of house. The installations in the foyer build on the audience enthusiasm for knowledge and deeper engagement with the work on stage.

During *War Horse*, for example, the team set up the biggest touch screen that had ever existed in the foyer area. With it, audience members could go behind the scenes, go into designer Rae Smith's sketchbook, and bring up discussions with the cast and production team.

Several shows on stage have focused on the impact of technology in daily life. *wonder.land*, that retelling of Lewis Carroll's classic story about Alice, relocated the story to an online game. Huge video projections displayed that curious, alternative world. In the foyer, the National's digital team created a series of games that audiences could play using gadgets – one headset even enabled them to visit the extraordinary psychedelic *wonder.land* themselves – so extending the world of the play out of the auditorium.

Ugly Lies the Bone by Lindsey Ferrentino told the story of a badly burned war veteran using virtual reality to reduce pain (it can impact the brain's capacity to notice pain and so reduce the sensation – sometimes even more effectively than powerful painkillers such as morphine). While the audience watched that process happening to the character on stage, in the foyer the team demonstrated the real-life software that the show was based on, so people could try it out after the show.

To boldly go

Theatre has always worked with new technology. As a storytelling organisation, we need find out what it means for how we can use it in our craft. Theatre is never an isolated discipline.

— Toby Coffey, Head of Digital Development

While much of the Immersive Storytelling Studio's work lies in augmenting performances by offering additional, complementary experiences, it is also occupied with exploring how such technology can be used with live theatre. In a sense, the two seem antithetical – theatre is live, communal and tangible whereas much of the digital world in particular involves solitary engagement. But proper, sophisticated fusion of the two can produce something that is exciting and worthwhile.

A successful example would be *Me and My Shadow*, a 2012 collaboration between the National Theatre and the dance collective body>data>space. This project encouraged members of the public to step into a large orb and move around or dance. As each person did so, motion capture technology created a purple silhouette on the orb that moved with them. But there were other silhouettes in different colours, also moving, also captured live. These were the avatars of people in other orbs in the cities of Paris, Istanbul and Brussels. Individuals could move their own silhouette to dance with those of others thousands of miles away. The show fused the roles of audience and performer and the worlds of live and virtual presence and was immensely popular.

Another fascinating project was *Draw Me Close*, a 2017 collaboration with the National Film Board Canada. This brought together live action, virtual reality and animation. An audience member would put on a headset in which they would see an illustrated version of the childhood home of film director Jordan Tannahill from the point of view of his five year-old self. They would then move around a specially constructed set. As they stretched out a hand to touch the illustrated door that they could see in their headset, they would feel a physical door handle, for example.

An actor wearing a live motion capture suit would join them in the space and become Jordan's mother in the illustrated version. When she interacted with the audience member, those moments would translate into the virtual illustration so that the person would feel her hugging them but experience that sensation through the eyes of the infant Jordan.

Those who encountered this show found it remarkable and moving. It also offered some insight into ways that new technology might work with live theatre to bring a new angle to the empathy and imagination that is at the heart of drama. The challenge is to make it work for a larger audience and in a way that is integral to the show, rather than as an add-on. The NT intends to keep pushing the boundaries of what live theatre means.

So while the Archive keeps touch with all that has happened at the National Theatre since its inception, new developments such as Public Acts, National Theatre Live, and the Immersive Storytelling Studio reach into the future and out of the building. In essence, they represent the latest attempts to examine what it means to be 'national' and what it means to make 'theatre' – questions that have preoccupied the directors, writers and actors of the NT since it was born. They are part of the rolling task to keep responding to Harley Granville-Barker's call all those decades ago for an ambitious, popular, inclusive institution that could become 'the property of the nation'.

Further Reading

Balancing Acts, Nicholas Hytner, Jonathan Cape, 2017

Concrete Reality, Patrick Dillon, National Theatre Publishing, 2015

Confessions of an Actor, Laurence Olivier, Orion, 1994 (first published Weidenfeld and Nicolson, 1982)

Dramatic Exchanges: The Lives and Letters of the National Theatre, edited by Daniel Rosenthal, Profile Books, 2018

Making an Exhibition of Myself, Peter Hall, Oberon Books, 2000 (first published Sinclair-Stevenson, 1993)

National Service: Diary of a Decade at the National Theatre, Richard Eyre, Bloomsbury, 2003.

All About Theatre, Marina McIntyre, Walker Books, 2015

The National Theatre Story, Daniel Rosenthal, Oberon Books, 2013

The National, A Dream Made Concrete, Peter Lewis, Methuen 1990

Olivier, Anthony Holden, Weidenfeld and Nicolson, 1988

Peter Hall's Diaries: The Story of a Dramatic Battle, Peter Hall, edited by John Goodwin, Oberon Books 2000 (first published Hamish Hamilton, 1983)

Stage Blood, Michael Blakemore, Faber and Faber, 2013

Author acknowledgements

I would like to thank all the very many creative artists, members of staff, heads of department, experts, technicians and makers working at the National Theatre for their invaluable help, patience and generosity in compiling this book: without them and their expertise, it would have been impossible to write. I am immensely grateful to Harry Scoble, Publishing Director, and Alison Rae, Head of Tours and Visiting, for their support and guidance. I am also particularly indebted to Daniel Rosenthal's brilliant and comprehensive history, *The National Theatre Story*, Patrick Dillon's beautifully detailed account of the building, *Concrete Reality*, and the BBC's vivid 2013 *Arena* documentary celebrating the National Theatre's 50th anniversary.

National Theatre acknowledgements

The intention of this book has been to offer a glimpse into the world of the National Theatre. There are so many people and departments involved in what we do that it has been impossible to include them all in these pages but they all perform vital functions in supporting our work here on the South Bank, nationally and internationally. We would like to thank everyone from:

The Board; The Associates of the National Theatre; The Senior Management Team; Archive; Audiences and Marketing; Box Office; Communications; Graphic Design Studio; Marketing; Press; Casting; Commercial and Media; Broadcast; Digital Development; Company Management; Stage Management; Development; Directors' Office; Enterprises; Audience Experience; Enterprises Finance; Food and Drink; Hospitality Events; House Management; Retail; Stage Door; Support Services; Tours and Visiting; External Relationships and Partnerships; Finance and Governance; Human Resources; Medical/ Welfare; Information Technology; Learning; Major Projects; New Work; NT Productions; Producing and Planning; Music, Production; Publishing;

Safety; Security; Armoury and Special Effects; Automation; Costume Production; Costume and Props Hire; The Drawing Office; Facilities; Lighting; Props; Rigging and Scenic Logistics; Scenic Construction and Scenic Art; Sound and Video; Stage; Stage Engineering; Technical Administration; Voice; Wardrobe; Wigs, Hair and Make-up; The American Associates of the National Theatre and NT America.

Image credits

p6	Philip Vile
p14	Zefrog/Alamy Stock
p20	Philip Vile
p30	Brinkhoff/Mögenburg
p34	Mike Smallcombe
p41	National Theatre Archive
p42	Philip Carter
p42	Philip Carter
p44	Helen Maybanks
p47	Mike Smallcombe
p51	Johan Persson
p54	Manuel Harlan
p59	Philip Vile
p60	Marc Brenner
p64	Angus McBean
p76	Kerry Harrison
p84	Kerry Harrison
p88	Marc Brenner
p94	Steve Tanner
p95	Steve Tanner
p100	Richard Hubert Smith
p104	Steve Tanner
p114	Mark Doet
p118	Johan Persson
p128	Kerry Harrison
p128	Kerry Harrison
p134	Simon Annand
p140	Ellie Kurttz
p146	Seamus Ryan
p150	Seamus Ryan
p156	Lucy Barriball
p162	Claire Nicholson
p162	Claire Nicholson
p164	Brinkhoff/Mögenburg
p176	Steve Tanner
p178	James Bellorini
p189	Helen Maybanks

INDEX

Page numbers in *italics* refer to illustrations.

R

S